BE DECISIVE

Be Decisive

WARREN W. WIERSBE

While this book is intended for the reader's personal enjoyment and profit, it is also intended for group study. A leader's guide with Reproducible Response Sheets is available from your local bookstore or from the publisher.

VICTOR BOOKS
A DIVISION OF SCRIPTURE PRESS PUBLICATIONS INC.
USA CANADA ENGLAND

Unless otherwise indicated, all Scripture references are from the *Authorized (King James) Version;* other references are from *The New King James Version* (NKJV). © 1979, 1980, 1982, Thomas Nelson, Inc., Publishers; the *Holy Bible, New International Version®* (NIV). Copyright © 1973, 1978, 1984 by International Bible Society. Used by permission of Zondervan Publishing House. All rights reserved; the *New American Standard Bible* (NASB), © the Lockman Foundation 1960, 1962, 1963, 1968, 1971, 1972, 1973, 1975, 1977; the *Revised Standard Version of the Bible* (RSV), © 1946, 1952, 1971, 1973; and *The Living Bible* (TLB), © 1971, Tyndale House Publishers, Wheaton, IL 60189. Used by permission.

Editors: Jerry Yamamoto, Barbara Williams
Design: Grace K. Chan Mallette
Cover Photo: Linde Waidhofer
Study Questions: Lin Johnson

Library of Congress Cataloging-in-Publication Data

Wiersbe, Warren W.
Be decisive / Warren W. Wiersbe.
p. cm.
Includes bibliographical references (p.).
ISBN 1-56476-489-3
1. Bible. O.T. Jeremiah—Commentaries. I. Title.
BS1525.3.W54 1995
224'.207—dc20

95-710
CIP

4 5 6 7 8 9 10 Printing/Year 05 04 03 02 01 00

CONTENTS

PRELUDE

"Power tends to corrupt and absolute power corrupts absolutely."

Lord John Acton wrote that in a letter to his friend Mandell Creighton on April 5, 1887. When he ended the letter, the British historian added this postscript: "History provides neither compensation for suffering nor penalties for wrong."

As you study the prophecy of Jeremiah, you'll learn that Lord Acton was right in his first statement; for you will meet in this book some of history's most powerful and corrupt rulers. But Lord Acton was terribly wrong in his postscript. God is still on the throne and history is His story. The German writer Friedrich von Logau said it better:

> Though the mills of God grind slowly, yet they grind exceeding small;
> Though with patience He stands waiting, with exactness grinds He all.

God judges the nations and eventually pays them the wages earned from their sin. No nation can despise God's law and defy His rule without suffering for it. The prophecy of Jeremiah teaches that very clearly.

In his familiar poem "The Present Crisis," the American poet James Russell Lowell penned words that summarize Jeremiah's life and ministry:

> Once to every man and nation comes the moment to decide,
> In the strife of Truth with Falsehood, for the good or evil side.

Though at first he hesitated when God called him, Jeremiah surrendered to the Lord and became one of history's most decisive spiritual leaders. Tragically, however, the people who most needed his leadership rejected him and turned their backs on the Word of God.

As never before, our homes, churches, cities, and nations need decisive leaders who will obey the Word of God. "If you ever injected truth into politics," quipped Will Rogers, "you have no politics." The politician asks, "Is it popular?" The diplomat asks, "Is it safe?" But the true leader asks, "Is it God's will? Is it right?" To quote James Russell Lowell's "The Present Crisis" again:

> Truth forever on the scaffold, Wrong forever on the throne,—
> Yet that scaffold sways the future, and, behind the dim unknown,
> Standeth God within the shadow, keeping watch above His own.

That's what the Lord told Jeremiah: "I am watching over My word to perform it" (Jer. 1:12, NASB).

Warren W. Wiersbe

A Suggested Outline of the Book of Jeremiah

Key Theme: Repent and return to the Lord or He will judge
Key Verse: Jeremiah 3:22

I. Jeremiah's call and commission—1

II. Jeremiah's messages to his people Judah—2–33
   1. During the time of Josiah's rule—2–13
      (1) The sins of the nation—2–6
      (2) The temple messages—7–10
      (3) The broken covenant—11–13
   2. The coming Babylonian invasion—14–16
   3. The Sabbath message—17
   4. The potter's house sermons—18–19
   5. Messages to the leaders—20–24
   6. Judah's captivity—25–29
   7. National restoration—30–33

III. Jeremiah's ministry and the fall of Jerusalem—34–39
   1. Ministry during the siege—34–38
      (1) To King Zedekiah—34, 37–38
      (2) To King Jehoiakim—35–36
   2. Jerusalem falls—39

IV. After the fall of the city—40–45, 52

V. Jeremiah's messages to the nations—46–51
   1. To Egypt—46
   2. To Philistia—47
   3. To Moab—48
   4. To Ammon, Moab, Edom, Syria, Kedar, and Elam—49
   5. To Babylon—50–51

ONE

JEREMIAH 1

The Reluctant Prophet

"For a people to boast in the glory of the past, and to deny the secret that made the past, is to perish."
—G. Campbell Morgan[1]

Jeremiah was perhaps twenty years old when God's call came to him in the thirteenth year of Josiah's reign (626 B.C.). Why did he hesitate to accept God's call? Let me suggest some reasons.

1. The task was demanding (Jer. 1:1)

Jeremiah's father Hilkiah was a priest,[2] as was his father before him, and young Jeremiah was also expected to serve at the altar. He may even have been at the age when he would have stepped into his place of ministry when God called him to be a prophet.

Since serving as a prophet was much more demanding than serving as a priest, it's no wonder Jeremiah demurred. If I had my choice, I'd take the priesthood! For one thing, a priest's duties were predictable. Just about everything he had to do was written down in the Law. Thus, all the priest had to do was follow instructions.[3] Day after day, there were sacrifices to offer, lepers to examine, unclean people to exclude from the camp, cleansed people to reinstate, official ceremonies to observe, a sanctuary to care for, and a Law to teach. No wonder some of the priests said, "Oh, what a weariness!" (Mal. 1:13, NKJV)

The ministry of a prophet, however, was quite another matter, because you never knew from one day to the next what the Lord would call you to say or do. The priest worked primarily to *conserve the past* by protecting and maintaining the sanctuary ministry, but the prophet labored to *change the present* so the nation would have a future. When the prophet saw the people going in the wrong direction, he sought to call them back to the right path.

Priests dealt with externals such as determining ritual uncleanness and offering various sacrifices that could never touch the hearts of the people (Heb. 10:1-18); but the prophet tried to reach and change hearts. At least sixty-six times the word "heart" is found in the Book of Jeremiah, for he is preeminently the prophet of the heart.

Priests didn't preach to the crowds very much but ministered primarily to individuals with various ritual needs. Prophets, on the other hand, addressed whole nations; and usually the people they addressed didn't want to hear the message. Priests belonged to a special tribe and therefore had authority and respect, but a prophet could come from any tribe and had to prove his divine call. Priests were supported from the sacrifices and offerings of the people, but prophets had no guaranteed income.

Jeremiah would have had a much easier time serving as a priest. Therefore, it's no wonder his first response was to question God's call. Offering sacrifices was one thing, but preaching the Word to hardhearted people was quite something else. When you read his book, you will see a number of pictures of his ministry that reveal how demanding it was to serve the Lord as a faithful prophet. In his ministry, Jeremiah had to be

- a destroyer and a builder – 1:9-10
- a pillar and a wall – 1:17-18
- a watchman – 6:17
- a tester of metals – 6:27-30
- a physician – 8:11, 21-22
- a sacrificial lamb – 11:19
- a long-distance runner – 12:5
- a shepherd – 13:17, 20-21; 17:16, 23
- a troublemaker – 15:10, 15-17

Does this sound like an easy task?

2. The times were difficult (Jer. 1:2-3; 2 Kings 21–25; 2 Chron. 33–36)

I suppose there never is a time when serving God is easy, but some periods in history are especially difficult for spiritual ministry, and Jeremiah lived in such an era. Consider what the history of Judah was like during Jeremiah's lifetime.

Rebellion instead of obedience. To begin with, Jeremiah was born during the reign of King Manasseh, the most evil man who ever reigned over the kingdom of Judah (2 Kings 21:1-18). The son of godly Hezekiah,[4] Manasseh came to the throne when only twelve years old, and the officials around him easily influenced him toward idolatry. Manasseh "seduced them [the people of Judah] to do more evil than the nations whom the Lord had destroyed before the Children of Israel" (v. 9, NKJV). When Manasseh died, his evil son Amon continued his father's evil practices.

Thus, Jeremiah grew up in Anathoth[5] at a time when idolatry flourished in Judah, children were offered in sacrifice to idols, the Law of Moses was disregarded and disobeyed, and it looked as though there was no hope for the nation. Godly priests were not greatly appreciated.

Reformation instead of repentance. In 639 B.C., some of Amon's servants assassinated him; Josiah his son became king, reigning until his untimely death in 609. Josiah was quite young when he began to reign, but he had godly counselors like Hilkiah, and thus he sought the Lord. In the twelfth year of his reign, he began to purge the land of idolatry; six years later, he commanded the priests and workers to repair and cleanse the temple. It was during that time that Hilkiah the priest found the Book of the Law in the temple and had it read to the king. This document may have been the entire five books of Moses or just the Book of Deuteronomy.

When the king heard the Law of God read, he was deeply moved. He tore his robes and sent to Huldah the prophetess for instructions from the Lord (2 Kings 22). Her message was that the people had forsaken God and therefore judgment was coming, but because of Josiah's sincere repentance, judgment would not come during his reign.

Josiah didn't wait for the temple repairs to be completed before calling the whole nation to repentance. He made a covenant with the Lord and led the people in renouncing idolatry and returning to the Law of the Lord. Unfortunately, the obedience of many of the people was only a surface thing. Unlike the king, they displayed no true repentance. Jeremiah knew this and boldly announced God's message: "Judah has not turned to Me with her whole heart, but in pretense" (Jer. 3:10, NKJV).

Josiah led the nation in a reformation but not in a heart-changing revival. The idols were removed, the temple was repaired, and the worship of Jehovah was restored, but the people had not turned to the Lord with their whole heart and soul.

Politics instead of principle. No sooner did Josiah die on the battlefield[6] and his son become king than the nation quickly returned to idolatry under the rule of Jehoahaz. But Pharaoh Necho removed Jehoahaz from the throne, exiled him to Egypt where he died, and placed his brother Eliakim on the throne, giving him the name Jehoiakim.

Jehoiakim, however, was no better than his brother and "did that which was evil in the sight of the Lord, according to all that his fathers had done" (2 Kings 23:37). He taxed the people heavily in order to pay tribute to Egypt, and then he agreed to pay tribute to Nebuchadnezzar, king of Babylon. After Jehoiakim reneged on that promise, Nebuchadnezzar took him prisoner to Babylon and took the temple vessels with him (597 B.C.).

Jehoiakim's son Jehoiachin reigned only three months; then his uncle Mattaniah, Josiah's third son (1 Chron. 3:15), was made king and renamed Zedekiah. Zedekiah was the last king of Judah, a weak, vacillating man who feared his officials more than he feared the Lord (Jer. 38:19).[7] "And he did that which was evil in the sight of the Lord his God, and humbled not himself before Jeremiah the prophet speaking from the mouth of the Lord" (2 Chron. 36:12). Zedekiah would ask Jeremiah for help while at the same time courting ambassadors from neighboring nations and plotting rebellion against Babylon. He allowed his princes to persecute and even imprison Jeremiah, though he himself had secret meetings with the prophet as if he were seeking God's will.

It's easy for political leaders to invite religious leaders in for consultation and then do exactly what they'd already planned to do. Today, it's good public relations to give people the impression that "religion" is important; but talking to a popular preacher isn't the same as humbling yourself before God.

Jeremiah preached to the nation for forty years, giving them God's promises and warnings; yet he lived to see Jerusalem and his beloved temple destroyed by Nebuchadnezzar's army and his people taken captive to Babylon. Jeremiah ministered in turbulent times and yet remained faithful to the Lord. He exposed the futile foreign policy of the rulers, pleading with them to turn to the Lord with all their hearts and trust God instead of trusting their political allies. Jeremiah is one of Scripture's greatest examples of faithfulness and decisive action in the face of physical danger and national decay.

3. The servant was doubtful (Jer. 1:4-10)

Jeremiah hesitated as he looked at the work before him and the wickedness around him, and when he looked at the weakness within himself, Jeremiah was certain that he wasn't the man for the job.

When it comes to serving the Lord, there's a sense in which nobody is adequate. "And who is sufficient for these things?" (2 Cor. 2:16) asked the great Apostle Paul as he pondered the responsibilities of ministry. Paul then answered his own question. "Not that we are sufficient of ourselves to think any thing as of ourselves; but our sufficiency is of God" (3:5).

When God calls us, however, He isn't making a mistake; and for us to hesitate or refuse to obey is to act on the basis of unbelief and not faith. It's one thing for us to know our own weaknesses, but it's quite something else for us to say that our weaknesses prevent God from getting anything done. Instead of being an evidence of humility, this attitude reeks of pride.[8]

God gave young Jeremiah three wonderful assurances.

God's electing grace (vv. 4-5). One of my seminary professors used to say, "Try to explain divine election and you may lose your mind, but explain it away, and you will lose your soul." God doesn't save us, call us, or use us in His service because we're deserving, but because in His wisdom and grace He chooses to do so. It's grace from start to finish. "But by the grace of God I am what I am," wrote Paul, "and His grace which was bestowed upon me was not in vain; but I laboured more abundantly than they all: yet not I, but the grace of God which was with me" (1 Cor. 15:10).

Each of the phrases in Jeremiah 1:5 is important. To begin with, God *knew* Jeremiah,[9] which refers to His sovereign election of His servant. God chose Jeremiah even before he was conceived or formed in his mother's womb. Then God *formed* Jeremiah and gave him the genetic structure He wanted him to possess. This truth is expressed poetically in Psalm 139:13-16. Jeremiah wasn't too happy about what his birth gave him (Jer. 20:14-18), but the Lord knew what He was doing. What we are is God's gift to us; what we do with it is our gift to Him.

God *sanctified* Jeremiah even before he was born. This means Jeremiah was set apart by the Lord and for the Lord even before he knew the Lord in a personal way. God would later do the same with Paul (Gal. 1:15). The Lord then *ordained* Jeremiah to be His prophet to the nations. God's concern from the beginning is that *all* nations of the earth know His salvation. That's why He called Abraham (Gen. 12:1-3) and set apart the nation of Israel to be His special channel to bring His Word and His Son into the world.

A prophet was a chosen and authorized spokesman for God who declared God's Word to the people. The Hebrew word probably comes from an Arabic root that means "to announce." For example, Moses spoke to Aaron, and Aaron was his spokesman (prophet) before Pharaoh (Ex. 7:1-2). Prophets did more than reveal the future, for their messages had present application to the life of the nation. They were *forth*tellers more than *fore*tellers, exposing the sins of the people and calling them back to their covenant responsibilities before God.

As God's children, we are chosen and set apart *by* Him and *for* Him (Eph. 1:3-14; Rom. 8:28-30); this truth ought to give us great courage as we confront an evil world and seek to serve the Lord. "If God be for us, who can be against us?" (Rom. 8:31)

God's protecting presence (vv. 6-8). God gave young Jeremiah three instructions: "Go where I send you, speak what I command you, and don't be afraid of the people." Then He added the great word of promise, "For I am with you to deliver you" (Jer. 1:8, NKJV). He repeated this promise at the end of His call: " 'They will fight against you, but they shall not prevail against you. For I am with you,' says the Lord, 'to deliver you' " (v. 19, NKJV).

Please note that there was a condition attached to this encouraging promise: Jeremiah had to go where God sent him and speak what God told him to speak. He also had to believe God's promise and prove it by not fearing the people. We call Jeremiah "the weeping prophet," and he was (9:1), but he was also a courageous man who faced many dangers and trials and remained true to the Lord. He knew that the Lord was with him, just as we should know that the Lord is with us. "For He Himself has said, 'I will never leave you nor forsake you.'[10] So we may boldly say: 'The Lord is my helper; I will not fear. What can man do to me?' " (Heb. 13:5-6, NKJV)

God's effecting Word (vv. 9-10). When the coal from the heavenly altar touched Isaiah's lips, it purified him (Isa. 6:5-7); when God's hand touched Jeremiah's mouth, it gave him power and authority. God put His words into the prophet's mouth and those words were effective to accomplish His will. God not only gave Jeremiah His words, but He also promised to "watch over" those words until they were fulfilled (Jer. 1:12).

The Word of God *created* the universe: "By the Word of the Lord the heavens were made, and all the host of them by the breath of His mouth. . . . For He spoke, and it was done; He commanded, and it stood fast" (Ps. 33:6, 9, NKJV). The universe is *upheld* by the Word of God: "And [Christ] upholding all things by the Word of His power" (Heb. 1:3, NKJV). But God also *carries out His purposes on earth* by means of His Word: "As the rain and the snow come down from heaven, and do not return to it without watering the earth and making it bud and flourish, so that it yields seed for the sower and bread for the eater, so is My Word that goes out from My mouth: It will not return to Me empty, but will accomplish what I desire and achieve the purpose for which I sent it" (Isa. 55:10-11, NIV).

In too many churches today, worship has become entertainment and preaching is merely the happy dispensing of good advice. We need to hear and obey Paul's admonition to Timothy, "Preach the Word" (2 Tim. 4:2). The Holy Spirit is the Spirit of truth (John 16:13) and works by means of the Word of truth (Ps. 119:43; 2 Tim. 2:15). Jeremiah didn't accomplish God's will on earth by means of clever speeches, cunning diplomacy, or skillful psychology. He heard God's Word, took it to heart, and then proclaimed it fearlessly to the people. God did the rest.

Jeremiah's ministry was difficult because he had to tear down before he could build, and he had to root up before he could plant. In too many ministries there are organizational "structures" that don't belong there and should be torn down because they're hindering progress. Some "plants" are taking up space but bearing no fruit, and they ought to be pulled up. Jesus said, "Every plant which My Heavenly Father has not planted will be uprooted" (Matt. 15:13, NKJV).

Any servant of God who feels himself or herself too weak to serve needs to consider these three encouragements. Has God called you? Then He will equip you and enable you. Are you obeying His commands by faith? Then He is with you to protect you. Are you sharing the Word? Then He will accomplish His purposes no matter how the people respond. Jeremiah's name means "Jehovah establishes," and God did establish His servant and his ministry and cared for him to the very end. "But the Lord is faithful, who will establish you and guard you from the evil one" (2 Thes. 3:3, NKJV).

4. The message was dangerous (Jer. 1:11-19)
When you study the Old Testament prophets, you discover that three strands of truth wove their messages together: (1) *past sin:* the nation has disobeyed God's Law; (2) *present responsibility:* the people must repent or God will send judgment; and (3) *future hope:* the Lord will come one day and establish His glorious kingdom.

The Lord didn't give Jeremiah a joyful message of deliverance to announce but rather a tragic message of judgment. So dangerous was this message that people hearing it called Jeremiah a traitor. He would be misunderstood, persecuted, arrested, and imprisoned; and more than once, his life was in danger. The nation didn't want to hear the truth, but Jeremiah told them plainly that they were defying the Lord, disobeying the Law, and destined for judgment.

God gave Jeremiah three promises to prepare him for this dangerous mission. Two of the promises were in visions.

The almond tree: God's Word will be fulfilled (vv. 11-12). In the Holy Land, the almond tree blossoms in January and gives the first indication that spring is coming. The Hebrew word for almond tree is *saqed,* while the word for "watch" or "be awake" is *soqed.* The Lord used this play on words to impress Jeremiah with the fact that He is ever awake to watch over His Word and fulfill it.

Like a husband or wife breaking the marriage vows, the sinful nation had turned from the covenant they had made with the Lord, and now they were giving their love and loyal ty to pagan idols. *But that covenant would stand, for the Lord had not forgotten it.* He had promised to bless them if they obeyed and chasten them if they disobeyed, and He was "watching to see that [His] word is fulfilled" (Jer. 1:12, NIV; see Lev. 26; Deut. 28). God had spoken to the nation through the earlier prophets, but the rulers and people wouldn't listen.

> Yet the Lord testified against Israel and against Judah, by all of His prophets, namely every seer, saying, "Turn from your evil ways, and keep My commandments and My statutes, according to all the Law which I commanded your fathers, and which I sent to you by My servants the prophets." Nevertheless they would not hear, but stiffened their necks, like the necks of their fathers, who did not believe in the Lord their God. And they rejected His statutes and His covenant that He had made with their fathers, and His testimonies which He had testified against them; they followed idols, became idolaters, and went after the nations who were all around them, concerning whom the Lord had charged them that they should not do like them (2 Kings 17:13-15, NKJV).

The boiling pot: God's wrath is coming (vv. 13-16). The nations in the East were often in conflict, each trying to gain supremacy. First the Jewish rulers would turn to Egypt for help, then to Assyria (see Isa. 30–31; Jer. 2:18, 36); and all the while, they failed to trust the Lord and seek His help. But this vision reveals that God is in control of the nations of the world and can use them to accomplish His own purposes. The Lord was even then preparing Babylon in the north[11] to be His servant to chasten His people. For Judah to turn to Egypt for help was futile because Egypt would also fall to Nebuchadnezzar (Jer. 46).

When Jeremiah began his ministry, Assyria, not Babylon, was the dominant power in the Near East, and no doubt many of the political experts thought Jeremiah foolish to worry about Babylon in the north. But the people of Judah lived to see Assyria defeated and Egypt crippled as Babylon rose to power and Jeremiah's words came true. Indeed, the thrones of the conquering Babylonian leaders were set in the gate of Jerusalem (39:1-3), and the holy city was eventually destroyed.

The sin God singled out was idolatry (1:16)—forsaking the true God and worshiping the gods they had made with their own hands. In their hypocrisy, the people of Judah maintained the temple worship, but Jehovah was only one of many gods who claimed their devotion. Some of the foreign idols were even brought into the temple! (See Ezek. 8–9.) The false prophets flourished in a ministry that was shallow and popular because they promised peace and never called for repentance (Jer. 5:12-13; 8:11-12; 14:13-22).

When a nation turns from worshiping the true God, its people begin to exploit one another, and that's what happened in Judah. The rich oppressed the poor and the courts would not defend the rights of the oppressed (2:34-35; 5:26-31; 7:1-11). Yet these evil rulers and judges went to the temple faithfully and pretended to be devoted to Jehovah! All they did was make the temple "a den of robbers" (7:11). It was this kind of sin that God was about to judge.

The city, pillar, and wall: God will protect His servant (vv. 17-19). In order to be able to run or work easily, men in that day had to tie their loose robes together with a belt (1 Kings 18:46; 2 Kings 4:29), so "gird up your loins" (Jer. 1:17) meant "Get ready for action!" It might be paraphrased "Tighten your belt! Roll up your sleeves!" "Gird up the loins of your mind" (1 Peter 1:13) means "Pull your mind together and have the right mental attitude in view of our Lord's return."

God repeated the warning He gave earlier (Jer. 1:8) that Jeremiah must not be afraid of the people who would oppose him, because God would defend him. Surrounded by his enemies, the prophet would become a fortified city they couldn't subdue. Forced to stand alone, Jeremiah would become as strong as an iron pillar. Attacked on all sides by kings, princes, priests, and people, he would be as unyielding as a bronze wall. "I am with you to deliver you" was God's reliable promise (vv. 8, 19, NKJV), and in the battle for truth, one with God is a majority.

In spite of the demands of the task and the difficulties of the times, Jeremiah accepted God's call. He knew his own deficiencies, but he also knew that God was greater and would enable him to do the job. The message God gave him was indeed dangerous, but God was watching over His Word to fulfill it and would protect His faithful servant.

Jeremiah made the right decision and as a result became one of the most unpopular prophets in Jewish history. Measured by human standards, his ministry was a failure, but measured by the will of God, he was a great success. It isn't easy to stand alone, to resist the crowd, and to be out of step with the philosophies and values of the times. Jeremiah, however, lived that kind of a life for over forty years.

In the final chapter of his book *Walden,* Henry David Thoreau writes: "If a man does not keep pace with his companions, perhaps it is because he hears a different drummer. Let him step to the music which he hears, however measured or far away."[12]

"If anyone desires to come after Me," said Jesus, "let him deny himself, and take up his cross, and follow Me. . . . For what is a man profited if he gains the whole world, and loses his own soul?" (Matt. 16:24, 26, NKJV)

In light of that sobering question, what decision will you make? Will you conform to the crowd or carry the cross?

TWO

JEREMIAH 2–6

The Prophet Preaches

"Nations, like individuals, are subjected to punishments and chastisements in this world."
—Abraham Lincoln[1]

In my library is a notebook containing the outlines of messages that I preached when I began my ministry back in 1950. Whenever I read those outlines, I feel very embarrassed and contrite in heart and I marvel that anybody ever listened to those sermons or came back to hear more. A seasoned preacher once said, "When you're young in the ministry, you can't understand why more people don't come to hear you. But when you get older, you're amazed that *anybody* comes to hear you." I agree.

Young Jeremiah, however, started his ministry with messages that were courageous, compassionate, and convicting.[2] Boldly he confronted the people with their sins and pled with them to repent and return to the Lord. Four major themes combine in these messages: rebellion, repentance, righteousness, and retribution.

THE PROPHET PREACHES

1. Rebellion: God sees His people's sins (Jer. 2:1-37)
Jeremiah had a gift for expressing theological truth in pictorial language. In fact, much of his preaching can be read as poetry.[3] In this chapter, he paints ten pictures that expose the sins of the people.

An unfaithful wife (vv. 1-8). When the Lord gave the Israelites His covenant at Mt. Sinai (Ex. 19–20), He entered into a loving relationship with them that He compared to marriage. "They broke My covenant, though I was a husband to them" (Jer. 31:32, NIV; see 3:14). In the Old Testament, Israel's idolatry is compared to adultery and even prostitution (see Isa. 54:5; Hosea 2:16). At the beginning of this covenant relationship, the Jews were devoted[4] to the Lord and loved Him, but once they conquered the Promised Land, their hearts lusted after the gods of the nations around them and they sank into idolatry (Jud. 1–3). Although God had taken them safely through their wilderness journey and given them a wonderful inheritance in Canaan, they abandoned Him for man-made gods. What kind of loyal love is that?

Broken cisterns (vv. 9-13). "Go from west to east," said the prophet, "and you will not find a nation that changed its gods." But Israel forsook the true God for false gods, which was like abandoning a spring of fresh flowing water for a cracked muddy cistern that couldn't hold water. In the Holy Land, water is a valuable possession, and nobody would do a foolish thing like that. No wonder the Lord said, "Be appalled at this, O heavens, and shudder with great horror" (Jer. 2:12, NIV). The second phrase literally means "Let your hair stand on end!"

A plundered slave (vv. 14-19). God redeemed the Jews from Egypt and gave them freedom in Canaan, but now their nation had gone back into bondage because of its idolatry. By allying with its pagan neighbors – Egypt and Assyria – instead of trusting the Lord, Judah had become a vassal state and was being plundered and enslaved. Instead of drinking at the pure river that the Lord gave them, the Judahites drank the polluted waters of the Nile and the Euphrates. Memphis and Tahpanhes were Egyptian cities, and Shihor was a branch of the Nile River.[5]

A basic principle is enunciated in verse 19: God punishes us by allowing our own sins to bring pain and discipline to our lives. "Your own conduct and actions have brought this upon you. This is your punishment. How bitter it is!" (4:18, NIV) "Your wrongdoings have kept these [rains] away; your sins have deprived you of good" (5:25, NIV). The greatest judgment God can send to disobedient people is to let them have their own way and reap the sad, painful consequences of their sins.

The word "backsliding" literally means "to turn away" and describes the nation's repeated apostasy.[6] The Book of Judges records at least seven occasions when Israel turned from the Lord and had to be chastened, and there were numerous other times during the period of the monarchy when the Israelites deliberately turned from the Lord. The word "backslide" is not used in the New Testament, but the experience is described in other ways: falling from grace (Gal. 5:4), leaving your first love (Rev. 2:4), loving the world (1 John 2:15-17; 2 Tim. 4:10), and walking in darkness (1 John 1:5-10).

A stubborn animal (v. 20). Jeremiah often used animals to picture the behavior of people, and here he compared the Jews to an unruly animal that won't wear the yoke.[7] One of his recurring phrases is "the stubbornness of their evil hearts" (3:17; 7:24; 9:14; 11:8; 13:10; 16:12; 18:12; 23:17, NIV).[8] When people, made in the image of God, refuse to obey God, they become like animals (see Ps. 32:9; Prov. 7:21-23; Hosea 4:16).

A degenerate vine (v. 21). Israel as a vine is a familiar image in the Old Testament (Isa. 5:1-7; Ps. 80:8-16; Ezek. 17:1-10; Hosea 10:1-2). God planted His people in the good land He gave them, but they didn't produce the harvest of righteousness He desired. "So He expected it to bring forth good grapes, but it brought forth wild grapes" (Isa. 5:2, NKJV). Because they worshiped false gods, they became like their degenerate neighbors. How could dead idols ever produce living fruit in their nation?

A defiled body (v. 22). No amount of good works or religious ceremonies could wash away their sins, because the heart of the nation's problem was the problem in their hearts. They had sinful hearts because they had stubborn hearts—hearts that refused to listen to God's servant and obey God's Word. Josiah's reformation was only a cosmetic change in the kingdom of Judah; it never reached the hearts of the people so that they repented and sought forgiveness from the Lord.

Jeremiah is preeminently the prophet of the heart, for he used the word over sixty times. "O Jerusalem, wash the evil from your heart and be saved" (Jer. 4:14, NIV). "The heart is deceitful above all things, and desperately wicked: who can know it?" (17:9) Judah needed to return to the Lord with their *whole* heart, for only then could He bless them.

An animal in the desert (vv. 23-25). Even if the people denied that they were defiled, their actions proved otherwise, for they were like animals: a lost camel, looking for an oasis; or a donkey in heat, running here and there, looking for a mate. As the Jews pursued the false gods of the pagan nations, their shoes wore out and their throats became dry. How much better had they drunk the refreshing water from the river of God!

But they had given themselves so much to sin that they despaired of being saved. "It's no use!" (2:25, NIV) was their excuse. "It's hopeless!" They sounded like confirmed alcoholics or compulsive gamblers who can't break the habit, or like the invalid at the Pool of Bethesda who had been sick for so long that he'd given up hope (John 5:1-9). *Jesus Christ, however, specializes in hopeless cases.* "He breaks the power of canceled sin/He sets the prisoner free."[9]

A disgraced thief (vv. 26-28). A thief caught in the act may protest his or her innocence, but the evidence is there for all to see. Any visitor to the kingdom of Judah could see what God saw: people turning their backs on God and talking to deaf idols, but then turning desperately to Jehovah for help when they found themselves in trouble. They were caught red-handed!

Incorrigible children (vv. 29-35). God chastened them many times for their sins, but they refused to change their ways, and then they even blamed God! He brought charges against them (Jer. 2:9), but instead of confessing and repenting, they complained and brought charges against Him! None of His discipline seemed to do any good. "You struck them, but they felt no pain; you crushed them, but they refused correction" (5:3, NIV; see 7:28; 17:23; 32:33; 35:13).

God reminded the people how richly He had blessed them. Yet they had rebelled against Him (2:29), forgot Him (v. 32), and lied to Him (vv. 33-35), claiming to be innocent. One of the major themes of the Book of Deuteronomy is that the nation remember the Lord and what He had done for them. Yet the people took their blessings for granted and gave their allegiance to dumb idols. They were so skilled at their harlotry, worshiping false gods, that even the most wicked prostitute could learn new things from them! They exploited the poor and were stained by their blood, and yet they pleaded innocent (see Amos 2:6-8; 5:10-12).

Because the nation at that time was enjoying a measure of political and economic prosperity, they concluded that God's blessing was proof of their innocence! They didn't realize that God can bless the wicked (Pss. 37 and 73; Matt. 5:45) and that the goodness of God should instead lead them to repentance (Rom. 2:4-5; Luke 15:17-18).

Prisoners of war (vv. 36-37). In its attempt to keep peace with its neighbors, Judah had flitted between Egypt and Assyria (Jer. 2:14-19), both of whom would ultimately disappoint Judah. The description in verse 37 is that of prisoners of war, their hands tied above their heads, being led away captive. Any decisions we make that are contrary to God's plan will lead to bondage, because only the truth can set us free (John 8:32). The Babylonian army would eventually overrun the land, take Jerusalem and destroy it, and lead the people away into captivity.

Was there any way Judah could escape the coming wrath? Yes, and that was the theme of the next point in Jeremiah's message.

2. Repentance: God pleads for His people to return to Him (Jer. 3:1–4:31)

The two key words in this section are "return" (3:1, 7, 12, 22; 4:1) and "backsliding" (3:6, 8, 11, 12, 14, 22). In the Hebrew, "backsliding" ("faithless," NIV) is actually a form of the word translated "return."

Pictures (3:1-10; 3:21–4:4). The prophet again used four vivid images to picture the sad spiritual condition of the kingdom of Judah.

THE UNFAITHFUL WIFE (3:1-10). Jeremiah returned to the metaphor of marriage that he had used in 2:1-2 and 20, but this time he introduced the subject of divorce. The Mosaic Law permitted a man to divorce his wife, but it did not allow him to marry her again (Deut. 24:1-4). God had every right to reject His people, because they had abandoned Him, not in order to marry another "husband," but in order to play the harlot with *many* lovers. The people had gone to the hills and built shrines dedicated to foreign gods. They had acted worse than common prostitutes who at least waited for lovers to come to them, for Judah had *pursued* false gods and repeatedly committed spiritual adultery with them.[10]

Instead of rejecting His people, however, the Lord patiently called for them to return and be restored as His wife. What grace! God had even caused a drought in the land, and the people had called out to Him for help (Jer. 3:4-5), but they had not really repented of their sins. Because of their covenant relationship with God, Judah called Him "Father" and "guide," which were titles Jewish wives sometimes used in addressing their husbands. But how could God give them covenant blessings when they were violating covenant commandments?

When Assyria conquered the Northern Kingdom of Israel in 722 B.C., the Southern Kingdom of Judah witnessed this divine judgment. Nevertheless, the Judahites refused to learn from Israel's destruction and turn from their sins (vv. 6-11). God had "divorced" Israel and put her away; Israel became a part of Assyria, and the Northern Kingdom was never restored. Having seen this judgment, the Judahites persisted in their sins as though it would never happen to them, and because of this arrogant attitude, Judah was even more guilty than Israel. Judah should have been "put away," yet God graciously invited His adulterous wife to return home to Him.

In obedience to the king, the people had cooperated with Josiah's reformation and outwardly put away their idols, but what they did was "only in pretense" (v. 10, NIV). God was "near in their mouth but far from their mind" (12:2, NKJV; see Ezek. 33:31). Even today, when political leaders claim to be born again and are willing to promote evangelical causes, going to church and reading the Bible become the "in" things to do, but you wonder how sincere these people really are. True Christian faith has never been popular, and the road that leads to life is still narrow and lonely (Matt. 7:13-23).

The Unhealthy Patient (3:21-25). In Scripture, sickness is one of many metaphors for sin (Jer. 8:22; 30:12; Isa. 1:5-6; Mark 2:17; Ps. 41:4). Like an infection entering the bloodstream, sin secretly gets into the system of the "inner man" and goes to work weakening and destroying. It gradually infects the whole system, producing spiritual lassitude and loss of spiritual appetite; and if not cared for, the "sin sickness" can lead to dire consequences. When we hear about believers "suddenly" falling into open sin, in most cases a gradual slide preceded the sudden fall.

God offers to heal, not just the symptoms of their backsliding, but the backsliding itself. The false prophets dealt only with symptoms and announced a false peace that gave the people a false confidence (Jer. 6:14; 7:8; 8:11). But a true physician of souls will tell the truth and seek to lead sinners to genuine spiritual healing that comes from honest confession and repentance.

This reminds me of a story I've often used in sermons. A certain church member was in the habit of closing his public prayers with "And, Lord, take the cobwebs out of my heart!" One of the other members became weary of this litany, so one evening, after hearing it again, he stood and prayed, "And, Lord, while You're at it . . . kill the spider!" Jeremiah was out to "kill the spider" and cure the patient.

The Jews thought their deliverance would come from the idols they worshiped in the high places—the hill shrines—but their only hope was to repent and trust the Lord.[11] These idols were unable to save them. In fact, they brought nothing but shame. Yet the Jews had sacrificed their God-given produce, flocks, and herds, and even their children to these shameful idols!

The Unplowed Field (4:1-3). The problem with the people was their dishonesty; they would use the right language, but they wouldn't mean it from their hearts. They would pray to the true God but not forsake the false gods. It was easy to say, "As the Lord lives," but they didn't say it "in truth, justice, and righteousness." Their hearts were hard and crowded with thorns like a neglected, unplowed field. Hosea used this image (Hosea 10:12) and so did Jesus in His Parable of the Sower (Matt. 13:1-9, 18-23).

THE UNCIRCUMCISED HEART (4:4). Jewish boys were circumcised when eight days old, given a name, and made a son of the covenant (Gen. 17:9-14; Lev. 12:3; Luke 1:59). Although no amount of surgery on the body could change the heart, the Jews thought that this ritual was their guarantee of salvation (Matt. 3:7-9; Acts 15:1-5). God, however, wanted them to "operate" on their hearts and put away their callousness and disobedience. "Therefore circumcise the foreskin of your heart, and be stiff-necked no longer" (Deut. 10:16, NKJV; see also 30:6; Rom. 2:28-29; Col. 2:11). They also needed to circumcise their ears (Jer. 6:10) so they could hear the Word of God.

Many people today depend on baptism, the Lord's Supper (Communion, the Eucharist), confirmation, or some other religious ritual for their salvation when what God wants from us is sincere faith from a repentant heart. Salvation is a gift that we receive by faith; it's not a reward that we earn by being religious.

Promises (3:11-13). The Lord even called to the dispersed Israelites to return to Him. This invitation reminds us of God's promises in Leviticus 26:40-45, Deuteronomy 30, and 2 Kings 8:46-53, which assured them that God would forgive if they would repent. In Jeremiah 3:14-19,[12] Jeremiah seemed to be looking far ahead to the Kingdom Age when Israel and Judah would be united, the nation would be purified and multiplied, and God would give them spiritual leaders to care for them. In the darkest days of their history, the Israelites heard their prophets announce this coming messianic kingdom, and the promise gave them hope.

The people must have been shocked when they heard Jeremiah say that the day would come when the ark of the covenant would be gone, forgotten, and never missed (v. 16). They trusted in the ark, the temple, the religious rituals, the covenant, and yet these things were but temporary signs that pointed to something spiritual and eternal.

The day would come when circumcised Jews would be treated like uncircumcised Gentiles (9:25-26), when the temple would no longer be needed (7:1-15; see John 4:20-24), and when there would be a new covenant that would change hearts (11:1-5; 31:31-40). Like Jesus, Jeremiah saw beyond external religion and taught that God was seeking the devotion of the heart. No wonder both of them were accused of being traitors and persecuted for opposing the "true religion," which God had given to Israel.

Punishment (4:5-18). Jeremiah announced the invasion of the Babylonian army from the north (1:14), like a fierce lion (4:7) and a devastating desert storm (vv. 11-13). Dreadful judgment was coming to Judah, and yet the nation was unprepared, because the people believed the deceptive message of peace proclaimed by the false prophets (v. 10).[13] "It can't happen here!" was their slogan. "After all, we have the temple and the ark of the covenant."

God commanded the watchmen to blow the trumpet and alert the people to run to the walled cities for safety. That would have given them time to repent in sackcloth (v. 8) and to wash their hearts by confessing their sins (v. 14). The Babylonian army, however, would come swiftly (v. 13; see Ezek. 38:16) and do their job thoroughly. "Your own conduct and actions have brought this upon you. This is your punishment. How bitter it is! How it pierces to the heart!" (Jer. 4:18, NIV).

Pain (4:19-31). Known as "the weeping prophet," Jeremiah

here expressed his personal anguish as he contemplated a national tragedy that could have been averted (4:19-21). No other Old Testament prophet revealed his brokenheartedness and sorrow as did Jeremiah (see 6:24; 9:10; 10:19-20). When ministering publicly, he was bold before men; in private, he was heartbroken before God.

God explained to His servant why the judgment was coming: The people were foolish; they did not know God; they were stupid; and they lacked understanding (4:22). If they had been as skillful in holy living as they were in sinning, God would have blessed them instead of judging them.

With prophetic vision, Jeremiah saw what the Babylonians would do to the land (vv. 23-29), producing chaos such as that described in Genesis 1:2.[14] No matter where he looked, he saw ruin. Even the stable mountains shook! It was only by the mercy of God that everything in Judah wasn't completely devastated (Jer. 4:27; see 5:10, 18; 30:11; 46:28).

But an equally great tragedy was the unbelief of the people who refused to repent and ask God for His help (4:30-31). Jeremiah described them as prostitutes who were trying to seduce other nations to come and help them stop the Babylonians, but their "lovers" wouldn't respond to their pleas. Judah trusted political alliances instead of trusting the Lord. But the prostitutes would become like women in travail—an image of painful judgment that's used often in Jeremiah (6:24; 13:21; 22:23; 30:6; 48:41; 49:22, 24; 50:43).[15]

3. Righteousness: God searches for the godly (Jer. 5:1-31)

Since the people would not listen to God's Word, God told Jeremiah to "act out" his message. This is the first of at least ten "action sermons" found in Jeremiah.[16] Meanwhile, this chapter deals with four sins of the people of Jerusalem.

Investigation: they were ungodly (5:1-6). God commanded Jeremiah to conduct a search of all the city of Jerusalem. If even one righteous person was discovered, the Lord would forgive the wicked city and call off the invasion. The background for this "action sermon" is God's agreement with Abraham to spare Sodom if ten righteous men were in the city (Gen. 18:22-33). The test in Jerusalem was, "Does the person practice justice and truth?"

Jeremiah found nobody among the poor who qualified, but he concluded that their lack of religious education would excuse them. The prophet then went to the nobles and the leaders, who he discovered knew God's commandments but threw off the yoke and turned away from the Law (Jer. 5:5; see 2:20; Ps. 2:1-3). When the survey was concluded, not one person was found who was honest and truthful.

One thing was left for God to do: He would allow the invaders to enter the land like marauding animals and destroy the people (see Jer. 2:15; 4:7). The animal had gotten loose from the yoke and run away from the master, only to be met by a lion, a wolf, and a leopard! What kind of freedom was that?

Condemnation: they were ungrateful (5:7-9). God asked two questions: "Why should I forgive you?" (v. 7, NIV) and "Shall I not punish them for these things?" (v. 9, NKJV) God "fed them to the full" (v. 7; "supplied all their needs," NIV), yet they used His gifts in order to commit sin and serve their idols. The goodness of God should have brought them to repentance (Rom. 2:4), but they were ungrateful for His blessings (Hosea 2:4-13). Instead of acting like men and women made in the image of God, they became like animals in heat ("well-fed, lusty stallions," Jer. 5:8, NIV; see 2:24).

The idolatrous nations in Canaan conducted a worship that was unbelievably immoral. In their minds, consorting with the temple prostitutes could guarantee a fruitful harvest. Baal was the storm god who provided the needed rain. Thus, when the Lord held back the rain to warn His people, they turned to pagan idols for help. Josiah had gotten rid of the temple prostitutes, but these prostitutes found other ways to carry on their trade and satisfy the desires they had inflamed in the men of Judah. Not unlike society today, the people worshiped sex and saw nothing wrong with what they were doing.

Devastation: they were unfaithful (5:10-19). This is the heart of the matter: Since the people did not believe God's Word, they turned their backs on God and went their own way. "They have lied about the Lord; they said, 'He will do nothing! No harm will come to us; we will never see sword or famine' " (Jer. 5:12, NIV). They rejected the Word God spoke through the prophets and called it "wind." As a result, God called for devastating judgment to come to His vineyard (vv. 10-11; see 2:21).

God, however, said His Word would be a fire that would consume the people like wood (5:14; see 23:29). Note the repetition of the phrase "eat up" ("devour," NIV) in 5:17, an announcement that the Babylonian invasion would consume the land and the people. This invasion would fulfill the warning given in Deuteronomy 28:49-52, a warning that the people knew. The Jews had forsaken the Lord and served idols in their own land. Now they would be temporarily forsaken by the Lord and taken to Babylon where they would serve idols in a foreign land.

Yet, this warning opened and closed with the promise that God would not destroy the nation completely (Jer. 5:10, 18; see 4:27; 30:11; 46:28).[17] Even in wrath, He remembers mercy (Hab. 3:2). The Jewish prophets announced judgment, but they also promised that a "remnant" would be spared. Isaiah repeated this promise (Isa. 1:19; 10:20-22; 11:11, 16; 14:22; 46:3) and even named one of his sons "a remnant returns" (Shearjashub, 7:3), and Micah echoed the same promise (Micah 2:12; 4:7; 5:3, 7-8; 7:18).

The remnant that returned to Judah from Babylon after the

Captivity restored the nation, rebuilt the temple, and maintained the testimony, preparing the way for the coming of the Messiah. God had covenanted with Abraham that through his descendants all the world would be blessed (Gen. 12:1-3), and God kept His promise.

Proclamation: they were unconcerned (5:20-31). Jeremiah was a retiring sort of person. Yet God told him to announce and proclaim boldly to the whole house of Jacob just what the people were like. The prophet's description of the people must have angered them, but it didn't shake them out of their complacency. Jeremiah told them that they were foolish, senseless, blind, and deaf, and that they had no fear of God. They were stubborn and rebellious, having turned away from serving the Lord. The mighty seas obeyed God's rule, but His own people rejected Him. God sent the rains and gave the harvests, but His people refused to thank Him.

Instead of encouraging one another to fear God, they exploited one another like hunters snaring birds. Thus the rich grew richer as the poor languished. The courts were corrupt, the prophets were liars, and the priests went right along with them; *and the people approved what was done and enjoyed it!* "My people love to have it so" (Jer. 5:31). When a nation becomes that corrupt, there is no hope.

The sinners thought they were getting away with their crimes, but God asked them, "What will you do in the end?" (5:31, NIV) "There is a way which seems right to a man, but its end is the way of death" (Prov. 14:12, NKJV).

4. Retribution: God sends His judgment (Jer. 6:1-30)

This closing section of Jeremiah's sermon focuses on the invading Babylonian army and the devastation they will bring to the kingdom of Judah. In that critical hour, the prophet told the nation what God was doing.

God declares war (vv. 1-5). First, the Lord spoke to His

people and warned them that judgment was coming (vv. 1-3). The Jews had three main ways to get military information: from the watchmen on the walls (v. 17), from trumpet signals (v. 1; see Num. 10:1-10), and from signal fires lit on high places (Jer. 6:1). Since Jeremiah's hometown of Anathoth was in Benjamin, he started by warning his own neighbors to get out of Jerusalem. Jerusalem is compared to a "beautiful and delicate woman," but she will end up like a "widow" (Lam. 1:1) with all of her beauty gone (v. 6). Foreign "shepherds" (soldiers) would invade the beautiful pastures and set up their tents only to slaughter the flock.

God then spoke to the Babylonian army over which He had command (Jer. 6:4-5), and He shared His strategy with them: make a surprise attack at noon, the hottest time of the day, when nobody would expect it, and plan to continue the attack through the night when most armies retire. The word translated "prepare" means "to sanctify or consecrate"; the Babylonians considered this war a holy crusade for their gods (see Joel 3:9; Micah 3:5).

God directs the attack (vv. 6-15). The Lord told the Babylonian army *what to do:* chop down trees and build ramps against the walls of the city. Then He told them *why* they were doing it. Jerusalem was like a well that pours out filthy water, and the city must be punished. It was like a dying person with infected wounds that couldn't be healed, and these things must be purged away. Finally, God told them *how to do it:* with precision and thoroughness, the way gleaners go over a vineyard so as not to miss any fruit (Jer. 6:5, 9).

The prophet lamented the fact that, at this critical time in history, *nobody was listening! (v. 10)* Not only were their hearts uncircumcised (4:4), but so were their ears (see Acts 7:51); and they refused to hear God's Word. Full of the wrath of the Lord, Jeremiah told them that God's anger will be poured out on young and old, men and women, and even the children. Rulers and priests won't escape; in fact, they were the most guilty because they had given the people false confidence and had refused to repent of their own sins (Jer. 6:13-15; see 7:8; 8:11). "For the sins of her prophets, and the iniquities of her priests" (Lam. 4:13) God would send this judgment.

God delivers the verdict (vv. 16-23). Are the people guilty? Yes! Do they deserve this punishment? Yes! In fact, God called the Gentiles and the earth to bear witness that He had done all He could to spare them this judgment (Jer. 6:18-19). They would not walk on His path,[18] and they would not listen to His prophets. Nevertheless, they continued to bring Him their hypocritical worship! (See Isa. 1:11-14; Amos 5:21; Micah 6:6-8.) God gave them the right way, but they rejected it. There could be no escape. The Babylonian army would be a formidable obstacle to anybody trying to flee the wrath of God. The daughter of Zion could not escape.

God describes the consequences (vv. 24-30). The prophet described the responses of the people as they heard the news—nothing but anguish, fear, and weakness, like a woman in hard labor (Jer. 6:24-26). "Terror on every side" (v. 25, NIV) is a phrase used again in 20:10, 46:5, and 49:29. This was the nickname Jeremiah gave Pashur, the chief officer of the temple (20:1-3).

Sometimes suffering brings out the best in people, but that wouldn't happen in the siege of Jerusalem. When God turned on the furnace, it would reveal the people as rejected silver, nothing but dross to be thrown away. He wasn't purifying them; He was punishing them. They weren't being refined; they were being rejected. They were too cheap to preserve.

"Indeed I tremble for my country when I reflect that God is just, and that His justice cannot sleep forever."

Thomas Jefferson wrote those words in his *Notes on the State of Virginia* over two centuries ago. It is still a sobering thought for us today.

THREE

JEREMIAH 7–10

The Voice in the Temple

"The more we know about the ancients, the more we find that they were like the moderns."
—Henry David Thoreau[1]

If there had been a newspaper published in Jerusalem in Jeremiah's day, successive editions in the year 609 B.C. might have carried headlines like these:

KING JOSIAH WOUNDED IN BATTLE!
Brave monarch brought to Jerusalem to recover

THE KING IS DEAD!
Jehoahaz succeeds father on throne

EGYPT DETHRONES JEHOAHAZ
Monarch reigned only three months

ELIAKIM IS NEW REGENT
Renamed "Jehoiakim" by Pharaoh

Behind these fictitious headlines were tragic events that hastened the decline and collapse of the kingdom of Judah. Zealous for the Lord, King Josiah had led the nation in a reformation during which he restored the temple buildings and removed the idols from the land. But in 609, he didn't heed God's warning and unwisely meddled in a war involving Egypt, Assyria, and Babylon. He was wounded in battle near Megiddo and taken to Jerusalem, where he died (2 Chron. 35:20-27). Though stunned by Josiah's death, the kingdom of Judah didn't see the loss of their king as God's call to national repentance and confession.

Josiah's son Jehoahaz reigned for three months, but was deposed by the king of Egypt and replaced by his brother Eliakim, whom the Egyptian king named "Jehoiakim." (Because of Josiah's defeat, Judah was now an Egyptian vassal state.) During Jehoiakim's eleven years' reign, he led the nation back into their old idolatrous ways. Although Josiah had removed the idols from the land, he couldn't take idol worship out of the hearts of the people.

The Jews didn't actually abandon the temple ministry; they simply brought their idolatry into the temple courts and made Jehovah one of the many gods they worshiped. If you had watched their worship, you would have thought the people were sincerely honoring the Lord; but their hearts belonged to Baal, Ashtoreth, Chemosh, and the other gods and goddesses of the heathen nations around them. Judah paid lip service to Jehovah but gave heart service to idols.

The Jews knew that idolatry was wrong, but they were confident they had nothing to fear. After all, God would *never* permit anything terrible to happen to the city where His holy temple was located! Didn't Judah possess the Law of Moses, and weren't the Jews the children of Abraham and the sons of the covenant? They were God's chosen people! With a religious heritage like that, no evil could ever fall on their kingdom!

God, however, had quite a different view of the matter. He commanded Jeremiah to go up to the temple and proclaim His message to the hypocritical people gathered there. In this courageous sermon, the prophet exposed the nation's *false worship* (Jer. 7:1–8:3), their *false prophets* (8:4-22), their *false confidence* in the covenant they were disobeying (9:1-26), and the *false gods* they were worshiping (10:1-25). In other words, Jeremiah dealt with their sinful mistreatment of the temple, the Law, the covenant, and the Lord Himself. It wasn't a popular message to deliver, and it almost cost him his life!

1. False worship: the temple (Jer. 7:1–8:3)

Three times a year, the Jewish men were required to go up to the temple in Jerusalem to celebrate the feasts (Deut. 16:16), and this may have been one of those occasions. The temple was probably crowded, but there weren't many true worshipers there. The prophet stood at one of the gates that led into the temple courts, and there he preached to the people as they came in. He presented God's four indictments against the people of Judah.

"Their worship does them no good" (vv. 1-15). Because they believed the lies of the false prophets, the people thought they could live in sin and still go to the temple and worship a holy God. According to Jeremiah 7:6 and 9, they were guilty of breaking at least five of the Ten Commandments, but the false prophets assured them that the presence of God's temple in Jerusalem guaranteed the nation God's blessing and protection from every enemy. Of course, this wasn't faith; it was blind superstition,[2] and Jeremiah quickly shattered their illusions.

Jesus referred to verse 11 after He cleansed the temple (Matt. 21:13). A "den of robbers" is the place where thieves go to hide after they've committed their crimes. Thus Jeremiah was declaring that *the Jews were using the temple ceremonies to cover up their secret sins.* Instead of being made holy in the temple, the people were making the temple unholy! A century earlier, Isaiah had preached the same message (Isa. 1); and much later Paul wrote a similar warning to Christians in his day (Eph. 5:1-7; Phil. 3:17-21). *Any theology that minimizes God's holiness and tolerates people's deliberate sinfulness is a false theology.*

The people needed to repent, not only to avoid the awful consequences of their sins in their character and their worship, but also to escape the judgment that was certain to come (Jer. 7:12-15). God's covenant with the Jews included both blessings and judgments, blessings if they obeyed and judgments if they rebelled (Deut. 11:26-30; 27:1-26; Josh. 8:30-35). Although the Jews knew this, they continued in their sins and rejected God's warning.

They also conveniently forgot God's past judgments, including His judgment on the tabernacle when it was located in Shiloh. The evil sons of Eli thought that carrying the ark of the covenant into the battle would defeat the Philistines, but they were slain, and the enemy captured the ark. God then wrote *Ichabod* over the tabernacle, which means in Hebrew "the glory has departed" (1 Sam. 4–6; see especially 4:21-22). Yes, God could protect His holy temple if He desired, *but His temple in Jerusalem was no longer holy.* It was a den of thieves! Better there was no temple at all than that hypocrisy should desecrate God's house.

"Your prayers will do them no good" (vv. 16-20). At least three times, God instructed Jeremiah *not* to pray for the people (Jer. 7:16; 11:4; 14:11)—certainly a terrible indictment against them. God had allowed Abraham to pray for wicked Sodom (Gen. 18:23-33), and He had listened when Moses interceded for sinful Israel (Ex. 32–33; Num. 14), but He wouldn't permit Jeremiah to plead for the kingdom of Judah. The people were too far gone in their sins, and all that remained for them was judgment (see 1 John 5:16; 1 Cor. 11:30).

When a nation decays, it begins in the home, and God saw whole families in Jerusalem working together to worship idols (Jer. 7:17-19). If only the parents had helped their children learn of the Lord and worship Him! The Jews, however, worshiped the "Queen of Heaven" which was a title for Ishtar, the Babylonian goddess of love and fertility, whose worship involved abominable obscenities (44:17-19, 25). This sinful worship certainly grieved God, but the people were hurting themselves more than they were hurting the Lord. This pagan immorality was having a devastating effect on their children, and God would send a judgment that would destroy the land, the city, the temple, and people. Judah was sacrificing the permanent for the immediate, and it was a bad bargain.

"Their sacrifices will do them no good" (vv. 21-26). A superficial reading of this paragraph may give the impression that God was denouncing the whole sacrificial system He had given to His people in Exodus and Leviticus, but such is not the case. In an ironic manner, Jeremiah was only reminding the people that the multitude of their sacrifices meant nothing because their hearts were unfaithful to God. God wants obedience and not sacrifice (1 Sam. 15:22), mercy and not religious rituals (Hosea 6:6). "Will the Lord be pleased with thousands of rams or with ten thousands of rivers of oil?" (Micah 6:7) asked the Prophet Micah. Then he answered his own question, "He has shown you, O man, what is good; and what does the Lord require of you but to do justly, to love mercy, and to walk humbly with your God?" (v. 8, NKJV; see Matt. 22:34-40)

God's covenant with Israel at Sinai emphasized the demonstration of His grace to the nation and the importance of their obedience to Him (Ex. 19:1-8). Jehovah was marrying a wife, not buying a slave. When Moses in Deuteronomy rehearsed the Law for the new generation, his emphasis was on loving the Lord and obeying Him from the heart (Deut. 6:1-15; 10:12-22; 11:1, 13, 22). To substitute external ritual for internal devotion would make the sacrifices meaningless and rob the heart of God's blessings. The same principle applies to believers today. How easy it is to be busy for the Lord and yet abandon our first love! (Rev. 2:4)

"My discipline and correction do them no good" (7:27–8:3). "This is the nation that has not obeyed the Lord its God or responded to correction" (Jer. 7:28, NIV). Whom the Lord loves, He chastens (Prov. 3:11-12; Heb. 12:5-13), and if we truly know and love the Lord, His chastening will bring us back to Himself in contrite obedience. But God told Jeremiah to lament for the dead nation, because they would not repent.

Topheth is an Aramaic word meaning "fireplace," and it sounds much like the Hebrew word meaning "shameful thing." Topheth was the place in the Valley of the Son of Hinnom where the people sacrificed their children to idols by throwing them into the fire (Isa. 30:33). King Josiah had defiled Topheth and turned it into a garbage dump (2 Kings 23:10), but after his death the gruesome pagan rituals were reinstated. The Greek word *gehenna,* meaning "hell," comes from the Hebrew *ge' hinnom,* "the valley of Hinnom." Hell is a garbage dump where Christ-rejecting sinners will suffer forever with the devil and his angels (Matt. 25:41).

Jeremiah announced that the day would come when the Valley of Hinnom would become a cemetery too small for all the people who would need burial after the Babylonian invasion. The army would plunder the graves and tombs, and the bones of the great leaders and kings would be desecrated on the altars like so many sacrifices to the gods they worshiped. Gehenna would again become a garbage dump, and the corpses of the Jerusalem citizens would be the garbage! "They will not be gathered up or buried, but will be like refuse lying on the ground" (Jer. 8:2, NIV).[3] Many of the people surviving the siege would be carried off to Babylon, and the land would become desolate.

2. False prophets: the Law (Jer. 8:4-22)

Having shattered the popular illusions about the temple, Jeremiah then exposed the false prophets who constantly opposed his ministry and led the people astray. He raised a number of questions in this section, but the whole proclamation centers on one major question: "Why did the nation not turn back to God?" In answering the question, Jeremiah dealt with three aspects of the people's stubborn refusal to obey God.

Their refusal was irrational (vv. 4-7). Jeremiah used analogies from human life and nature to illustrate his point. When people fall down, they get up again. That's the sensible thing to do. If they find themselves walking on the wrong path, they retrace their steps and get on the right path. Conclusion: if people can be sensible about these everyday matters, why can't they be sensible about eternal matters, especially since the consequences are much more tragic?

They were like horses rushing into battle, having no idea of the dangers involved. Horses are trained to obey and may not know any better, but people made in the image of God ought to know where they're going. In fact, the people of Judah weren't as smart as the birds! (See Isa. 1:3.) God gave the birds the instinct to know the seasons and the times of their migrations, but He gave people so much more: a spirit within to hear God's voice and understand His Law. Made in the image of God, men and women ought to be as obedient to divine instruction as birds are to natural instinct.

Their refusal was caused by deception (vv. 8-12). "Lo, they have rejected the word of the Lord; and what wisdom is in them?" (Jer. 8:9) Just as they boasted that they possessed the temple, so they boasted that they had the divine Law (v. 8), *but possessing the Scriptures isn't the same as practicing the*

Scriptures. Although the Bible is still a bestseller, its popularity isn't keeping Western society from crumbling morally and spiritually. There appears to be no connection between what people say they believe and the way people act.

The false prophets, who claimed to be writing and speaking in the name of the Lord, deceived the kingdom of Judah. They were men whose personal lives were godless, whose hearts were covetous, and whose remedies for the problems of the nation were useless. Their ministry was popular because they majored on the superficial and marketed whatever good news the people wanted to hear (see 5:12; 14:13-15; 27:8-9; 28:1-17). Jeremiah pictured these men as deceitful physicians (6:14; 8:11), empty wind (5:13), dispensers of chaff (23:28), ruthless, selfish shepherds (23:1-4), and infected people spreading disease (23:15, NIV). God had not sent these so-called prophets (14:14; 23:18, 21; 29:9, 31), nor did they receive their messages from God (23:25-28).

What happens to the Lord's people largely depends on the leaders they follow. Worldly leaders attract and produce worldly people, but you pay a price to follow spiritual leadership. It's much easier to drift with the current and go along with the crowd. Jeremiah had few friends or disciples because his message wasn't popular.

Their refusal would lead to judgment (vv. 13-22). These verses blend three voices: God's voice of judgment, the people's voice of despair, and the prophet's voice of anguish as he contemplated the ruin of a once-great nation. God declared that the fields would be ruined (vv. 13, 17), the cities would be destroyed (v. 17), and the people would be either slain or taken captive (v. 19). It would be like drinking poison (8:14; 9:15; 23:15), experiencing an earthquake (8:16), being attacked by venomous snakes (v. 17), or being crushed and broken (v. 21).

How did the people respond? Instead of turning to the

Lord, they fled to their walled cities! (v. 14) Their cry of despair was, "Where is the Lord? Why did He allow this to happen?" (see v. 19) But it happened because they were disobedient and unfaithful to the covenant they had made with the Lord. Their situation was hopeless; nobody would come to save them. Verse 20 was the proverb they quoted: "The harvest is past, the summer has ended, and we are not saved." *They had missed their God-given opportunity, and it would never come again.*

Since Jeremiah was a faithful shepherd, he identified with the hurts of the people: his heart fainted (v. 18) and he mourned in horror as he felt the heavy burden that was crushing the land. "For the hurt of the daughter of my people am I hurt" (v. 21). The false prophets had made a wrong diagnosis and prescribed the wrong remedy, and the wounds of the nation were still open, bleeding, and infected. "To the Law and to the testimony! If they do not speak according to this Word, it is because there is no light in them" (Isa. 8:20, NKJV).

3. False confidence: the covenant (Jer. 9:1-26)

The Jews are the only nation in history with whom God has entered into a covenant relationship (Gen. 12:1-3). As the children of Abraham, marked by the seal of circumcision (Gen. 17), they are indeed a "special people" to the Lord (Ex. 19:4-6). The tragedy is that they trusted the covenant and the ritual to guarantee them acceptance before the Lord. They thought they didn't need to repent or believe; that was for the "uncircumcised" Gentiles. John the Baptist faced this obstacle in his ministry (Matt. 3:7-10), and so did Jesus (John 8:33ff) and Paul (Rom. 2–4). Jeremiah had to deal with the pride of his people as he pointed out to them three obvious truths.

Being God's covenant people is no excuse for sin (vv. 1-6).

Like Jesus (Luke 19:41) and Paul (Rom. 9:1-5), Jeremiah wept over the sad spiritual condition of the people, and this is one reason he's known as "the weeping prophet" (see Jer. 9:18; 10:19; 13:17; 14:17; Lam. 1:16; 2:11, 18; 3:48). It's unusual today to find tears either in the pulpit or the pews; the emphasis seems to be on enjoyment. Instead of evangelists and revivalists, the church now has "religious comedians" who apparently have never read James 4:9-10, "Lament and mourn and weep! Let your laughter be turned to mourning and your joy to gloom. Humble yourselves in the sight of the Lord, and He will lift you up" (NKJV). Vance Havner was right: "Never in history has there been more ribald hilarity with less to be funny about."[4]

Jeremiah would rather have fled from the people to a place of peace (see Ps. 55:6), but he knew that his calling was to stay and minister God's Word (Jer. 40:6). His soul was grieved at the sins of the people, their immorality, idolatry, deception, and slander. Truth was a precious commodity; you couldn't even trust your friends and relatives!

The people of Judah thought they were "free to sin" because they'd been born children of Abraham and were the people of the covenant. On the contrary, being a part of God's covenant gave them a greater responsibility to live to glorify Him and obey His will! "Shall we continue in sin, that grace may abound? God forbid" (Rom. 6:1-2). As I said before, any theology that minimizes personal holiness and excuses sinfulness is not biblical theology.

Being God's covenant people offers no escape from judgment (vv. 7-16). If anything, their favored relationship with the Lord invited an even greater judgment; for "everyone to whom much is given, from him much will be required" (Luke 12:48, NKJV). God said to the Jews, "You only have I chosen of all the families of the earth; therefore I will punish you for all your sins" (Amos 3:2, NIV).

That punishment would be like the heat of a furnace (Jer. 9:7). It would leave the cities in ruins, places for animals to dwell; the fruitful fields would become like deserts because nobody would live there and cultivate them. So terrible would the devastation be that even the birds would flee because there would be no places for them to nest. Why would the "land of milk and honey" become a barren wilderness? Because the people disobeyed God's law and turned to idols. They thought their "favored status" before the Lord would protect them from judgment.

Being God's covenant people is no assurance of spiritual understanding (vv. 17-26). "Let not the wise man glory in his wisdom, let not the mighty man glory in his might, nor let the rich man glory in his riches; but let him who glories glory in this, that he understands and knows Me" (vv. 23-24, NKJV). No amount of education, power, or wealth—three things the world today depends on and boasts about—can guarantee the blessing of God. God doesn't delight in a nation's learning, political influence, armies, or gross national product. He delights in a people who practice kindness, justice, and righteousness because they know and fear the Lord. God promises covenant blessings to those who obey Him, not to those who only submit to religious ceremonies.

God called the nation to lament because they would soon be going to their own funeral. Death was coming, and the politicians and false prophets wouldn't be able to hinder it. Death is pictured as a thief who comes unhindered through the windows to steal precious lives. Bodies would fall "like cut grain behind the reaper" (v. 22, NIV).[5]

The Jews boasted in the covenant sign of circumcision, but it was only in their flesh; the true spiritual circumcision had never reached their hearts (4:4; Deut. 10:16; Acts 7:51; Rom. 2:25-29). People today who depend on baptism and other church sacraments (ordinances), but who have never repented and trusted Christ, are in the same situation as the Jews in Jeremiah's day; they think they're a part of the divine covenant, but their confidence is a false one. Paul was a good example of this: he had to lose his religious righteousness in order to gain Christ! (Phil. 3:1-11)

4. False gods: the true and living God (Jer. 10:1-25)

Before Abraham trusted in the true God, he had been a worshiper of idols (Josh. 24:2-3). During their years in Egypt, the Jews were exposed to the gross idolatry of that land, and some of it stayed in their hearts. While Moses was meeting with God on Mt. Sinai, the people, aided by Moses' brother Aaron, made a golden calf and worshiped it (Ex. 32). At Sinai, they had seen the glory of God, heard the voice of God, and accepted the Law of God; yet "they changed their glory into the image of an ox that eats grass" (Ps. 106:20, NKJV). Idolatry was in their hearts.

Jeremiah looks around and ridicules the idols (vv. 1-16). Instead of separating themselves from the evil practices of the nations, as Moses had instructed (Deut. 7:1-11), Israel gradually imitated those practices and began to worship pagan gods. But these gods were worthless, manufactured by craftsmen, "like a scarecrow in a melon patch" (Jer. 10:5, NIV). They can't speak or walk, and they have to be carried around (see Ps. 115). If only the people would contemplate the glory and majesty of the true and living God—the everlasting God who created the heavens and the earth by the Word of His power!

A.W. Tozer reminds us that "the essence of idolatry is the entertainment of thoughts about God that are unworthy of Him."[6] It means worshiping and serving the creature rather than the Creator (Rom. 1:25), the gifts rather than the Giver. The idols were senseless, and so were the people (Jer. 10:8), because we become like the god we worship (Ps. 115:8).

Our contemporary idols aren't ugly as were the pagan idols in Jeremiah's day, but they capture just as much affection and do just as much damage. Whatever we worship and serve other than the true and living God is an idol, whether it's an expensive house or car, the latest stereo equipment, a boat, a library, a girlfriend or boyfriend, our children, a career, or a bank account. That on which I center my attention and affection and for which I am willing to sacrifice is my god, and if it isn't Jesus Christ, then it's an idol. "Little children, keep yourselves from idols" (1 John 5:21).

The remedy for idolatry is for us to get caught up in the majesty and grandeur of God, the true God, the living God, the everlasting king. An idol is a substitute, and you would never want a substitute once you have experienced the love and power of the Lord God Almighty.

Jeremiah looks ahead and laments the judgment that is coming (vv. 17-22). Jeremiah saw the invasion of the Babylonian army and the distress they would bring. He urged the people to pack their bags and get ready to move, because they would be hurled out of the land like stones from slings. The prophet lamented the ruin of houses and families, the separation of parents and children, the scattering of God's precious flock.

Jeremiah pointed out the reason for this disaster: the shepherds (political and spiritual leaders; KJV "pastors") didn't seek the Lord but instead led the people astray (Jer. 10:21). The judgment came "for the sins of her prophets, and the iniquities of her priests" (Lam. 4:13). A nation went into captivity because their leaders forsook the true and living God.

Jeremiah looks up and prays for mercy (vv. 23-25). God had instructed Jeremiah not to pray for the nation (Jer. 7:16); so he didn't. Instead, he prayed for himself as a representative of the nation. Once again, he identified with the pain of the people (10:19). This prayer presents three arguments to persuade the Lord to be merciful to His people.

First, God must remember that they are only weak humans who don't know how to run their own lives (v. 23). Jeremiah may have been thinking of Psalm 103:13-16.

Second, if God gave them what they deserved, they would be destroyed (Jer. 10:24). Again, Psalm 103:10 comes to mind: "He has not dealt with us according to our sins, nor punished us according to our iniquities" (NKJV). As Ezra expressed it, God punishes us "less [than] our iniquities deserve" (Ezra 9:13).

His third argument was that the nations attacking Judah deserved punishment for seeking to destroy God's chosen people (Jer. 10:25). God called Babylon to be His tool to *chasten* the Jews, not to wipe them out, but the Babylonians were ruthless in their treatment of Judah. The prophet wasn't giving vent to his own personal wrath; he was pleading for the Lord to keep His promises to Abraham and protect the nation from extinction (Gen. 12:1-3). God answered that prayer and eventually brought an end to the savage rule of Babylon (see Jer. 50–51).[7]

It was on this note that Jeremiah ended his "temple sermon." The results? According to Jeremiah 26, he was seized and condemned to die! Rather than hear and obey the true Word of God, the priests would rather commit murder! The Lord saved Jeremiah from being killed, but he was banished from the temple (36:5). I wonder how many preachers today would boldly preach a message they knew would result in their being dismissed? And I wonder how many in the congregation would be willing to accept that message and obey it?

God didn't promise Jeremiah an easy ministry, but He did promise to keep him strong (1:7-8, 17-19). He kept His promise to Jeremiah, and He will keep His promises to His servants today.

FOUR

JEREMIAH 11–13

Voting with God

> *"Whoso who would be a man must be a nonconformist."*
>
> —R.W. Emerson[1]

In his poem "The Need of the Hour," the American poet Edwin Markham wrote:

We need the faith to go a path untrod,
The power to be alone and vote with God.

That's what Jeremiah was doing during the reign of King Josiah: walking alone and voting with God. King Josiah was excited when the workmen repairing the temple found the Book of the Law (2 Kings 22), and this discovery led to a movement that temporarily cleansed the kingdom of idolatry (2 Kings 23). This event is commonly called "Josiah's revival," but "reformation" might be a more accurate word. Why? Because the people obeyed the Law only outwardly; in their hearts they still held onto their idols.

Because Jeremiah understood this and knew the shallowness of the unrepentant human heart, he wasn't too vocal during Josiah's reformation.[2] He knew what the people were doing in secret and that they would return to their sins at the first opportunity. In this section of his prophecy, Jeremiah recorded the sins of the nation and pleaded with the people to return to the Lord while there was yet time.

1. Breaking God's covenant (Jer. 11:1-8)

The king and the people had publicly promised the Lord that they would obey the terms of His covenant (2 Kings 23:3), and there's no question that the king was sincere. With most of the people, however, their obedience was only a matter of going along with the crowd and doing what was popular.

The history of the Jews is the record of covenants: God made them and the people broke them. He made a covenant with Abraham when He called him to leave Ur and go to Canaan (Gen. 12:1-3), and He confirmed this covenant with Isaac (26:1-5) and Jacob (35:1-15). The Abrahamic Covenant is the basis for all the blessings Israel has received from the Lord.

At Sinai, God entered into another covenant with Israel, one that involved obedience to His holy Law (Ex. 19–20). "Now therefore, if you will indeed obey My voice and keep My covenant, then you shall be a special treasure to Me above all people; for all the earth is Mine" (19:5, NKJV). The people agreed to obey the Lord (v. 8), but it didn't take long for them to disobey. While they were still at Sinai, they made an idol and worshiped it (Ex. 32).

Before Israel entered the land of Canaan, Moses reviewed the covenant (the Book of Deuteronomy) and reminded the people of their obligations to the Lord. Their *ownership* of the land depended on God's promise to Abraham, but their *possession* and *enjoyment* of the land depended on their obedience to God's Law. Moses reviewed the blessings and the curses (Deut. 27–28); later, Joshua reaffirmed them in the Promised Land (Josh. 8:30-35). The Jewish people knew that God would bless them if they were true to Him and that He would chasten them if they were disobedient.

The land of Egypt had been an "iron furnace" to Israel (Jer. 11:4), a place of suffering (Deut. 4:20; 1 Kings 8:51; Isa. 48:10); but Canaan was "a land flowing with milk and honey" (Jer. 11:5), a place of prosperity and freedom. God described the Promised Land to Moses in this way (Ex. 3:8, 17; see 33:3), and Moses repeated this description to the people (Lev. 20:24; Deut. 6:3; 11:9; 26:9, 15; 27:3; 31:20). Sad to say, the nation preferred the fleshpots of Egypt to the milk and honey of Canaan (Ex. 16:3; Num. 11:4, 34) and repeatedly wanted to go back to Egypt.

During Josiah's reformation when the nation seemed to be turning back to the Lord, God commanded Jeremiah to go through the streets of Jerusalem and declare the terms of His covenant to the people. Both God and Jeremiah knew that the nation's obedience wasn't from the heart. No matter what they were doing in the temple, the people were still visiting the high places and honoring the gods of the nations around them.

The Prophet Ezekiel described their sin perfectly when he wrote, "Son of man, these men have set up their idols in their heart" (Ezek. 14:3). A century earlier, Isaiah had described Judah's empty hypocritical worship, comparing Jerusalem to Sodom and Gomorrah (Isa. 1:10ff). The people brought abundant sacrifices, but God didn't need them or want them. Their incense was an abomination, their annual feasts were sinful activities, and God hated it all and was tired of it. "If you are willing and obedient, you shall eat the good of the land; but if you refuse and rebel, you shall be devoured by the sword" (Isa. 1:19-20, NKJV).

God told Jeremiah to remind the people of both the blessings and the curses written in the covenant. If God's blessings couldn't motivate them to obey His commandments, perhaps the fear of God's judgment might cause them to obey. God had to treat His people like little children who obey either to get a reward or to escape a spanking. How He longed for them to obey because they loved Him and wanted to please Him![3]

Jeremiah answered "So be it!" (Jer. 11:5) to God's words, which is the way Israel was supposed to respond to God's covenant (see Deut. 27:9-26; Josh. 8:30-35). But the prophet was walking alone; the people weren't interested in doing the will of the Lord. Had the nation repented and turned humbly to the Lord, the people could have averted the terrible judgment brought by the armies of Babylon. As it was, their hypocrisy made that judgment only worse.

2. Conspiring against God's authority (Jer. 11:9–12:6)
The Lord revealed to His servant a twofold conspiracy in the land: a conspiracy of the men of Judah to disobey the covenant and resist the reforms led by King Josiah (11:9-17), and a conspiracy of the people in Jeremiah's hometown to kill the prophet and silence God's Word (11:18–12:6). Both led to a third crisis that threatened Jeremiah's own faith in the Lord.

The conspiracy against the king (vv. 9-17) was actually a hidden rebellion against God's covenant and the reforms that Josiah was bringing to the land. Unless the Word of God is obeyed and worked out practically in our lives, God can't bless us as He desires to do. The people, however, preferred to break the covenant and worship false gods.

But *what* we worship and *the way* we worship are not incidentals in life; they're essentials that determine the character of life itself. "A people's lives are only as good as their worship," writes Eugene Peterson. "Worship defines life. If worship is corrupt, life will be corrupt."[4] God gave His people the covenant so He might bless them and keep the good promises He made to them, but His people preferred to trust the gods of their pagan neighbors.

Worship has consequences, either good or bad, and in the case of Judah, the consequences were bad. The people knew that the curses and judgments were written into the covenant, but they thought God wouldn't send judgment on His own chosen people. Wasn't God's temple in Jerusalem? Wasn't the ark of the covenant there? And didn't the priests have the Law? Would God allow these sacred things to be destroyed? But God always keeps His promises, whether to bless or to chasten, and the greater the privileges we have from Him, the greater the responsibility we have to Him.

Disaster was coming to Judah and nothing could change it. The people could cry out to their gods, but their gods wouldn't answer them. Even if the people turned back to Jehovah and begged for His help, He wouldn't answer them. Therefore, the Lord commanded Jeremiah a second time not to pray for the people (11:14; see 7:16; 14:11). The people worshiped as many gods as there were cities in Judah, and there were as many altars as streets in Jerusalem. Yet none of these things could rescue the nation from the terrible judgment that was coming.

God presented two pictures of His people that reveal how futile their religious faith really was: a worshiper in the temple (11:15) and a tree in the storm (vv. 17-18). God called the nation "my beloved," reminding them of their marriage contract and how unfaithful they had been to Him. Their worship in the temple should have been an expression of their true love to Him, but instead it was an exercise in futility. Offering sacrifices could never avert God's judgment; the people were merely engaging in wickedness (v. 15, NIV). When worship becomes wickedness, and people rejoice in sinning, then the light has turned into darkness (Matt. 6:22-24), and there is no hope.

In Scripture, trees sometimes symbolize individuals (Jer. 17:8; Pss. 1:3; 52:8; 92:12; Zech. 4:3) and sometimes nations or kingdoms (Isa. 10:33-34; 18:5; Ezek. 17; 31). Israel is compared to an olive tree in Jeremiah 11:16-17, an image Paul used in Romans 11. The olive tree is prized in the Near East because of its fruit and the useful oil made from it. Judah thought of herself as a "thriving olive tree" (Jer. 11:16, NIV) that would never fall, but God saw a storm coming, and the wind would break the branches and the lightning would set the tree on fire. Jerusalem would be broken down and burned like a useless olive tree.

If the greatest sin is the corruption of the highest good, then Judah was guilty of great sin. Their highest good was to know the true God and worship Him, but they perverted that blessing and worshiped idols. They turned His temple into a den of thieves, persecuted His prophets, rejected His covenant, and disgraced His name. "God's name is blasphemed among the Gentiles because of you" (Rom. 2:24, NIV; see Ezek. 36:22). God patiently dealt with His people, seeking to woo them back, but they only hardened their hearts and turned a deaf ear to His warnings.

Before we condemn the people of Judah, however, let's examine our own hearts and churches. Are there idols in our hearts? Do we give wholehearted devotion to the Lord, or is our devotion divided between Christ and another? When unsaved people visit our worship services, are they impressed with the glory and majesty of God? (1 Cor. 14:23-25) Do the worldly lives and questionable activities of professed believers disgrace God's name? Remember, God's "last word" to the church isn't the Great Commission; it's "Repent, or else!" (Rev. 2–3)

The conspiracy against Jeremiah (vv. 18-23) grew out of the people's rejection of God's Word, for if they had accepted the Word of God, they would have honored His prophet and listened to what he had to say. You would think that the priests in Anathoth would have had more discernment than to listen to the false prophets, but holding a religious office is no guarantee that people possess spiritual wisdom.

The men of Anathoth, Jeremiah's hometown, plotted to kill him because his message convicted them. Rather than repent, they decided to destroy the messenger. But they had a second reason: as loyal Jews, they felt that his prophecies were harmful to the welfare of the nation. Jeremiah preached impending judgment from Babylon, while the false prophets were declaring messages of peace (Jer. 6:14; 8:11). Jeremiah insisted that the people obey the law and bring their sacrifices to the temple and not to the local shrines ("high places"), some of which were dedicated to idols, and the priests didn't like that. Jeremiah was pro-Babylon while the rulers were pro-Egypt. In other words, Jeremiah was out of step with his times, and because he was decisive, he had to walk alone and "vote with God."

Until God warned him about it, Jeremiah knew nothing about the plot against his life, and when he heard the news, he felt like a helpless lamb being led to the slaughter (11:19; see Isa. 53:7). All he could do was commit himself and his enemies to the Lord and trust God to work. This is the first of several occasions in his life when Jeremiah privately poured out his heart to the Lord and asked Him to fight his battles and help him with his depression and fears (Jer. 11:19-20; 12:1-4; 15:10-17; 17:12-18; 18:20-23; 20:7-18). Publicly, Jeremiah was bold before people, but privately, he was broken before God. God assured His servant that his enemies would be dealt with when the day of disaster came and the Babylonians captured Jerusalem.

A theological crisis followed (vv. 1-6). No sooner did God take care of the two conspiracies than Jeremiah found himself struggling with a theological crisis (12:1-6). "In the commencement of the spiritual life," wrote the French mystic Madame Guyon, "our hardest task is to bear with our neighbor; in its progress, with ourselves; and in its end, with God." Jeremiah couldn't understand why a holy God would permit the false prophets and the unfaithful priests to prosper in their ministries, while he, a faithful servant of God, was treated like a sacrificial lamb.

"Why does the way of the wicked prosper?" (v. 1, NIV) is a question that was asked frequently in Scripture, and it's being asked today. Job wrestled with it (Job 12; 21); the psalmists tried to understand it (Pss. 37; 49; 73); and other prophets besides Jeremiah grappled with the problem (Hab. 1; Mal. 2:17; 3:15). Jewish theologians, pointing to the covenants, taught that God blesses those who obey and judges those who disobey, but the situation in real life seemed just the opposite! How could a holy God of love allow such a thing to happen?[5]

Jeremiah, however, was seeking more than answers to questions; he was also concerned for the welfare of his people. He saw the land distressed because of the sins of the leaders, with many innocent people suffering. God had sent drought to the nation, which was one of the covenant disciplines (Deut. 28:15-24), and the vegetation was withering and the animal life dying. But the evil leaders who were to blame for the drought were not only surviving but also were prospering from the losses of others.

This didn't seem fair, and Jeremiah complained to the Lord. "Why do all the faithless live at ease?" (Jer. 12:1, NIV) "How long will the land lie parched?" (v. 4, NIV) "Why?" and "How long?" are questions that are easy to ask but difficult to answer.

Jeremiah's suggested solution was that God judge the wicked and drag them away like cattle to be slaughtered (v. 3). After all, the men of Anathoth were ready to slaughter him like a sacrificial lamb (11:19). So why shouldn't they receive from God the same fate they had planned for him?

God's reply to Jeremiah, however, wasn't what he expected (12:5-6). *God's focus was not on the wicked; it was on His servant Jeremiah.* As most of us do when we're suffering, Jeremiah was asking, "*How* can I get out of this?" But he should have been asking, "*What* can I get out of this?" God's servants don't live by explanations; they live by promises. Understanding explanations may satisfy our curiosity and make us smarter people, but laying hold of God's promises will build our character and make us better servants.

God's reply revealed three important truths to Jeremiah. First, *the life of godly service isn't easy;* it's like running a race. (Paul used a similar figure in Phil. 3:12-14.) Had he remained a priest, Jeremiah probably would have had a comfortable and secure life, but the life of a prophet was just the opposite. He was like a man running a race and having a hard time keeping going.

Second, *the life of service becomes harder, not easier.* Jeremiah had been running with the foot soldiers and had kept up with them, but now he'd be racing with the horses. In spite of his trials, he'd been living in a land of peace. Now, however, he'd be tackling the thick jungles of the Jordan River, where the wild beasts prowled. His heart had been broken because of the attacks of outsiders, but now *his own family* would start opposing him.

The third truth grows out of the other two: *the life of service gets better as we grow more mature.* Each new challenge (horses, jungles, opposition of relatives) helped Jeremiah develop his faith and grow in his ministry skills. The easy life is ultimately the hard life, because the easy life stifles maturity, but the difficult life challenges us to develop our "spiritual muscles" and accomplish more for the Lord. Phillips Brooks said the purpose of life is the building of character through truth, and you don't build character by being a spectator. You have to run with endurance the race God sets before you *and do it on God's terms* (Heb. 12:1-3).

"It was the answer Jeremiah needed," said Scottish preacher Hugh Black. "He needed to be braced, not pampered."[6]

One of my relatives, when a boy, deliberately failed third grade so he wouldn't have to go into fourth grade *and write with ink!* Today, our grandchildren are learning to use simple computer programs in grade school so they'll be prepared to use more difficult programs in high school and college. There's no growth without challenge, and there's no challenge without change. As they get older, many people resist change, forgetting that without the challenge of change, they're in danger of deteriorating physically, mentally, and spiritually. God wanted Jeremiah to grow, and He also wants us to grow.

Gilbert K. Chesterton put it this way: "The fatal metaphor of progress, which means leaving things behind us, has utterly obscured the real idea of growth, which means leaving things inside us."[7] God was concerned about the development *within* the prophet, not just the difficulties around him. God could handle the problem people in Judah, but God couldn't force His servant to grow. Only Jeremiah could make that choice by staying in the race, accepting new challenges, and thereby maturing in the Lord.

3. Ignoring God's warnings (Jer. 12:7–13:27)

God used what Jeremiah said and did to speak to the people of Judah and warn them of the terrible judgment that was coming. Comfortable in their false confidence and encouraged by the false prophets, the leaders and people of Judah were living in a fool's paradise, certain that nothing terrible could happen to either the holy city or the temple. Note the eight vivid images that depict the judgment that was about to fall.

The rejected inheritance (vv. 7-17). The people of Israel were God's special inheritance (Ex. 19:5-6; Deut. 4:20; 32:9), and the land of Canaan was their inheritance from Him (Ex. 15:17; Ps. 78:55). The land belonged to the Lord and was only "loaned" to the Jews for them to use (Lev. 25:23). The people were to obey the laws that protected the land from abuse and defilement, but they disobeyed those laws and defiled their inheritance (Lev. 18:25, 27; Deut. 21:23). God disciplined them by taking them out of the Promised Land and deporting them to Babylon. This gave the land of Israel opportunity to be healed (2 Chron. 36:21; Jer. 25:9-12; Lev. 26:34-43).

You can't miss the anguish of God's heart as He spoke concerning His beloved people. Instead of loving Him, they were roaring at Him like an angry lion, and He couldn't express His love to them as He yearned to do.[8] Judah's enemies were like birds of prey and wild beasts, just waiting to attack. The leaders of those nations ("shepherds"; "pastors") and their armies would turn the beautiful vineyard into a wasteland, and the Jewish people would be uprooted from their inheritance. The people of the neighboring nations—Syria, Moab, and Ammon—who had attacked Judah in the past would also be punished by Babylon, and some of them would also be taken captive.

The Lord, however, added a word of hope: "I will return, and have compassion on them, and will bring them again, every man to his heritage, and every man to his land" (Jer. 12:15). The people would be in captivity for seventy years (25:11-12; 29:10) and then be permitted to return to their land and restore their temple and nation. God would invite the people of the other nations to worship Him—the true and living God—and they would no longer teach His people how to worship false gods.

The marred waistcloth (vv. 1-11). This was one of Jeremiah's "action sermons."[9] The waistcloth was a thigh-length undergarment worn next to the skin. God had brought the nation close to Himself, but they had defiled themselves with idols and become "good for nothing." When the people saw Jeremiah bury his new garment under a rock in the muddy river, they knew it would ruin the garment, but they didn't realize they were passing judgment on themselves. God would one day take Judah to Babylon, and there He would humble the Judahites and cure them of their idolatry. The city and temple that they were proud of would be ruined, just as the prophet's garment had been ruined.

But something else was involved in this "action sermon." For years, the leaders of Judah had turned to Egypt, Assyria, and Babylon for help, instead of turning to the Lord, and this "help" had only defiled them and made them "good for nothing" in God's sight. Jeremiah was showing them that their "flirting" with the pagan nations was only alienating them further from the Lord and that it would ultimately end in national ruin.

The staggering drunkards (vv. 12-14). Jeremiah used a familiar proverb as his text: "Every [wineskin][10] shall be filled with wine" (13:12). The proverb expresses the assurance that there will be peace and prosperity for the nation, not unlike the American proverb, "A chicken in every pot."[11] With a broken heart, the prophet saw the leaders getting drunk when they should have been soberly seeking the Lord (see Isa. 28:1-8), and he knew that a cup of wrath was about to be poured out on the land (Jer. 25:15ff). The leaders and the people of Jerusalem were filling their jars with wine, preparing for a party, but God would fill them with a drunkenness that would lead to shameful defeat and painful destruction. They would crash into one another and destroy one another like clay pots smashed in a siege. Paul used the image of drunkenness to admonish the church to be ready for the Lord's return (1 Thes. 5:1-11).

The stumbling traveler (vv. 15-16). When Jeremiah called to the people, "Hear ye and give ear [pay attention]!" (Jer. 13:15) he was giving them opportunity to repent and turn to the Lord. He compared them to a traveler on an unfamiliar and dangerous mountain trail, without a map and without light, hoping for the dawn. Instead of the light dawning, however, the darkness only deepens. In centuries past, God had led His people by a pillar of cloud and fire. Now He wanted to lead them through the words of His prophet, but the people wouldn't follow. *If we reject God's light, nothing remains but darkness.* The leaders were too proud to admit they were lost, and they wouldn't ask for directions.

The captive flock (vv. 17-20). Jeremiah wept as he saw the Lord's flock being taken captive, defenseless sheep heading for the slaughter. What caused this great tragedy? The shepherds (rulers of Judah) selfishly exploited the sheep and refused to obey the Word of the Lord (23:1ff). Jeremiah spoke to King Jehoiachin and Nehushta, the queen mother (2 Kings 24:8-20), and admonished them to repent and humble themselves, but they refused to listen. Babylon would swoop down from the north and the nation would be ruined. "Pride goes before destruction, and a haughty spirit before a fall" (Prov. 16:18, NKJV).

The woman in travail (v. 21). This is a familiar biblical image of suffering, and it's usually associated with judgment (Jer. 4:31; 6:24; 22:23; 30:6; 49:24; 50:43; 1 Thes. 5:3). The message of the verse is "The people you sought as allies will come and be your masters. Then what will you say? You'll be so gripped with pain that you won't be able to say anything." Had they looked to Jehovah as their ally, He wouldn't have failed them, but they trusted Babylon, and Babylon turned out to be their enemy.

The disgraced prostitute (vv. 22-23, 26-27). According to the Law of Moses, prostitution was not permitted in the land (Lev. 19:29; 21:7, 14), and public exposure sometimes disgraced the prostitutes. If a prostitute discovers herself stripped, shamed, and abused, why should she be surprised? That's what she asked for! The people of Judah prostituted themselves to heathen idols and turned to godless nations for help. Now they were asking, "Why have all of these things happened to us?" People may live as though sin has no consequences, but those consequences will come just the same. Just as Ethiopians can't change the color of their skin, or the leopard remove its spots, so the wicked nation can't naturally do anything good. These people are too accustomed to committing evil. Only God can change the human heart.

The blown chaff (vv. 24-25). God compared the wicked nation to chaff that will be blown away (Ps. 1:4; see Matt. 3:12). Chaff is the useless by-product of the harvesting process. The workers throw the grain into the air, and the desert wind blows the chaff away. Sin had so cheapened the kingdom of Judah that the people were worthless, fit only to be blown away. They forgot their Lord, believed lies, and would not repent of their sins.

How patient the Lord was with His people, and how patient His servant was to minister to them! Jeremiah was willing to walk alone and "vote with God" so his people might have an opportunity to be saved, but they spurned his message.

God is still "long-suffering to us-ward, not willing that any should perish, but that all should come to repentance" (2 Peter 3:9). Unlike the people of Judah, let's listen to His Word and obey Him; for only then can we escape His discipline and enjoy His blessings.

FIVE

JEREMIAH 14–17

Sermons, Supplications, and Sobs

"Our modern age is a pushover for the shallow and the shortcut. We want to change everything except the human heart."

—J. Wallace Hamilton[1]

Preaching that costs nothing accomplishes nothing."[2]

The famous British preacher John Henry Jowett made that statement, and it certainly applies to the Prophet Jeremiah. Pained by the sins of his people, declaring unpopular messages that majored on judgment, and perplexed by what the Lord was allowing him to suffer, Jeremiah paid a great price to be faithful to his divine calling. If ever an Old Testament servant had to "take up his cross" in order to follow the Lord, it was Jeremiah.

In these chapters, the prophet delivered four messages, and interspersed with these messages were his own prayers to the Lord and the answers he received. Jeremiah was bold before men but broken before God, and yet it was his brokenness that gave him his strength.

1. A message about the drought (Jer. 14:1-22)
Unlike the land of Egypt whose food supply depended on irrigation from the Nile River, the land of Canaan depended on the rains God sent from heaven (Deut. 11:10-12). If His people obeyed His Law, God would send the rains[3] and give them bumper crops (Lev. 26:3-5), but if they disobeyed, the heaven would become like iron and the earth like bronze (Lev. 26:18-20; Deut. 11:13-17; 28:22-24). Over the years, Judah's sins had brought a series of droughts to the land[4] (see Jer. 3:3; 5:24; 12:4; 23:10), and Jeremiah used this painful but timely topic as the basis for a sermon to the people.

The plight of the land (vv. 1-6). Whether in the cities (14:1-3), the farms (v. 4), or the open country (vv. 5-6), no matter where you looked throughout Judah, you found suffering and privation. The land was in mourning and its citizens were lamenting, like people at a funeral. Because of the sins of the people, God was withholding the life-giving rains and thus keeping His covenant promise to Israel. It made no difference how rich you were, there wasn't any water to be found. The rivers were dry, the cisterns were empty, and both the servants in the cities and the farmers in the country covered their heads like people in a funeral procession. Even the animals were suffering because of the sins of the people. The doe, usually faithful to her young, abandoned her newborn fawn to starve to death, and the wild donkeys, their eyes glazed, could only stand on the barren heights and pant hopelessly for water.

It's a serious thing to enter into a covenant relationship with God, because He will always keep His Word, either to bless or to chasten. If we are the recipients of His love, then we can expect to be the recipients of His chastening if we disobey Him (Prov. 3:11-12). God is always faithful.

The plea of the people (vv. 7-12). As people usually do when they're in trouble, the Jews turned to God and prayed, but their prayers were insincere and not linked with repentance. Jeremiah had already confronted these pious hypocrites with their sins when he asked, "Will you steal, murder, commit adultery, swear falsely, burn incense to Baal, and walk after other gods whom you do not know, and then come and stand before Me in this house which is called by My name, and say, 'We are delivered to do all these abominations?' " (Jer. 7:9-10, NKJV)

Because they couldn't plead for help on the basis of their repentance and God's covenant promise (Deut. 30:1-10; 2 Chron. 7:12-15), the people of Judah asked God to help them for His own name's sake. "After all," they argued, "it's Your reputation that's at stake, because we're called by Your name." The Hope and Savior of Israel was like a tourist in the land, unconcerned about either its present condition or its future destruction. The Lord was like a person shocked into paralysis or a warrior completely without strength.

When God disciplines us, it isn't enough that we pray and ask for His help; anybody in trouble can do that. We must repent of our sins, judge and confess them, and sincerely seek the face of God. To weep because of the sufferings that sin causes is to show remorse but not repentance. "Rend your heart, and not your garments" (Joel 2:13) was the Prophet Joel's counsel to the Jews during another time of great calamity; and David, when he sought God's forgiveness, said, "The sacrifices of God are a broken spirit: a broken and a contrite heart, O God, Thou wilt not despise" (Ps. 51:17).

God responded to the people's words, not by sending rain, but by announcing judgment! (Jer. 14:10) For the third time, He told His servant Jeremiah not to pray for the people (v. 11; see 7:16; 11:14). His long-suffering had run out, and He was determined to punish them for their sins. They could fast, pray, and bring sacrifices, but nothing would change His mind. The nation was destined for the sword, famine, and pestilence (14:12). The Babylonian army would bring the sword, and the results of its devastating invasion would be famine and pestilence.[5]

The protest of the prophet (vv. 13-16). "But is it really the fault of the people?" Jeremiah asked. "Aren't the people being led astray by the false prophets who are promising them deliverance and peace? *They* are the real culprits" (see 5:12; 6:14; 8:11). God agreed that the prophets were leading the people astray through their false visions and lies, and He assured Jeremiah that these people would suffer for what they had done. The day would come when they and their families would be slain and nobody would bury their corpses—one of the most humiliating things that could happen to a Jew.

The people, however, *were* responsible for their actions because they should have known that the Lord had not sent these prophets. There were two tests of a true prophet or prophetess in Israel: (1) their predictions were 100 percent accurate (Deut. 8:20-22),[6] and (2) their messages agreed with the Law of God (13:1-18). *Any prophet who permitted the worship of idols, contrary to God's Law, was a false prophet.* "To the Law and to the testimony: if they speak not according to this word, it is because there is no light in them" (Isa. 8:20). Even if a professed prophet performed miracles, he or she was a counterfeit if God's revealed truth in the Word did not support the message. Miracles are no guarantee of a divine call (2 Thes. 2:7-12).

The pain and prayer of the prophet (vv. 17-22). How did Jeremiah feel about his people? The same way God felt: he wept for them (Jer. 9:18; 13:17), the way a father would weep for a virgin daughter who had been violated, beaten, and left to die. In prophetic vision, the prophet saw the land ravaged and the people taken captive to Babylon (14:18), and this led him to turn to God in prayer.

Since Jeremiah had been commanded not to pray *for* the nation (14:11), he identified himself *with* the people and used the pronouns "we" and "us," not "they" and "them" (see Neh. 1:4-10; Ezra 9; Dan. 9; Rom. 9:1-3). In praying for himself, he was praying for them; and he asked God to honor His own name and keep His covenant by sending healing to the land. Although God was certainly willing to keep *His* part of the covenant, the people weren't willing to keep their part. Therefore, the prophet's prayer went unanswered. A faithful God cannot violate His own Word.

Sometimes God permits disasters to occur to bring nations, churches, and individuals to their knees in repentance. The plagues of Egypt should have made Pharaoh a contrite man, but he only hardened his heart even more against the Lord (Ex. 7–12). Israel's treatment of the nations in Canaan was God's judgment because these nations refused to turn from their sins (Gen. 15:16; see Dan. 8:23; Matt. 23:32-35). While we shouldn't interpret every calamity as an expression of divine wrath, we must be sensitive to God and be willing to search our hearts and confess our sins.

2. A message about the coming Captivity (Jer. 15:1-21)
Before the Jews even entered the Promised Land, Moses had rehearsed with them the terms of the covenant, warning them that He would remove them from the land if they refused to obey His voice (Deut. 28:63-68). No sooner did Joshua and that generation of spiritual leaders pass from the scene (Jud. 2:7-15) than the nation turned to idolatry and God had to chasten them. First, He punished them *in the land* by allowing other nations to invade and take control. Then, when the people cried out for help, He raised up deliverers (vv. 16-23). By the time of Jeremiah, however, the sins of the people were so great that God had to remove them *from the land* and punish them in distant Babylon.

Two responses are recorded in this chapter: the Lord's response to Jeremiah's prayer (Jer. 15:1-9), and Jeremiah's response to the Lord's answer (vv. 10-21).

The Lord's response to Jeremiah's prayer (vv. 1-9). No matter who sought to intercede for Judah, God's mind was made up, and He would not relent. At critical times in Jewish history, Moses and Samuel had interceded for the people, and God heard and answered (Ex. 32–34; Num. 14; 1 Sam. 7; 12; Ps. 99:6-8). But God's heart would go out to the people no longer. Instead, His people would go out into captivity. "Send them away from My presence! Let them go!" (Jer. 15:1, NIV)

The people faced four possible judgments: death from disease, war, starvation or, if they survived these calamities, exile in Babylon.[7] The bodies of those slain by the Babylonian army would be desecrated and eaten by dogs, birds, or wild beasts; none would have a decent burial. It wasn't a bright future that God revealed to His people, but it was a future they themselves had chosen by refusing to repent of their sins. You take what you want from life and you pay for it.

God had chosen the Jews to be a blessing to the nations of the world (Gen. 12:1-3), but now they would become "abhorrent to all the kingdoms of the earth" (v. 4, NIV; see 24:9; 29:18; 34:17; Deut. 28:25), an object of scorn, "a byword among the nations" (Ps. 44:14, NIV). Not only that, but Jerusalem and the land itself would bear witness to God's judgment of their sins. "Their land will be laid waste, an object of lasting scorn; all who pass by will be appalled and will shake their heads" (Jer. 18:16, NIV; see 19:8; 25:9, 18; 29:18).

One of the causes for this terrible judgment was King Manasseh, who reigned for fifty-five years (697–642) and was the most wicked king in Judah's history (2 Kings 21:1-18; 2 Chron. 33:1-10). He was the son of godly Hezekiah and the grandfather of godly Josiah, and yet he himself was an evil man who encouraged Judah in the sins that brought about the downfall of the kingdom. God wasn't punishing the nation for the sins Manasseh committed but because the nation imitated Manasseh in their sinning.

In fact, the Lord lamented over the suffering that would come to His people because of their disobedience (Jer. 15:5-9). Would anybody pity Jerusalem or even ask about her welfare? Nehemiah did (Neh. 1:1-3), and centuries later, Jesus wept over the city (Matt. 23:37). For God to postpone judgment would have meant encouraging the nation's sins even more, and this He would not do. He was "weary with repenting" (Jer. 15:6).[8]

The coming judgment would be like separating wheat from the chaff (v. 7; see 51:2). The wives would become widows, and the mothers would be bereaved of their sons. A woman with seven sons would be considered especially blessed, but if all of them were killed in battle, it would be as though the sun went down at noon, cutting the day short. The light of her life would be gone because the future of the family had been destroyed.

We must not think that God enjoyed sending judgment to His people. If He has no pleasure in the death of *the wicked* (Ezek. 18:23, 32), He certainly has no pleasure in the death of *His own people!* God is long-suffering, but when His people resist His gracious call and rebel against His will, He has no alternative but to send chastening.

Jeremiah's response to the Lord's message (vv. 10-21). This is the third of Jeremiah's recorded laments (see 11:18-23). If the mothers of the dead soldiers had reason to weep (Jer. 15:8-9), Jeremiah's mother had even more reason, for the people treated him as though he were the enemy. The soldiers died as heroes, but Jeremiah lived as if he were a traitor to his own people. Jeremiah wasn't a creditor, pressuring his borrowers. Nevertheless, everybody hated him. God promised to deliver him (v. 5), and He kept His promise, but God didn't promise to shield him from persecution. Jeremiah was now running with the horses, and it wasn't easy (12:5).

In resisting Nebuchadnezzar, Judah was fighting a losing battle, for nothing could break "the northern iron" of Babylon. Judah would lose its treasures and become slaves of the Babylonians. This wasn't a popular message to proclaim, and Jeremiah knew it would arouse the opposition of the leaders and the people. Therefore, he asked God for the help he needed to keep going. His requests were "Remember me, care for me, and avenge me of my enemies."

Jeremiah 15:15-18 reveals the turmoil that was in the prophet's heart and mind. One minute he was affirming the Lord's long-suffering and his own faithfulness to the Word,[9] and the next minute he was crying out with pain because of the suffering of his people and the difficulty of his work. He even suggested that God had lied to him when He called him and that God was "like a deceptive brook, like a spring that fails" (v. 18, NIV; see Job 6:15-20).

Jeremiah was human and had his failings, but at least he honestly admitted them to God. Instead of piously covering up his true feelings, he poured out his heart to the Lord, and the Lord answered him. God's answer may have shocked the prophet, for the Lord told him he needed to repent! "If you repent, I will restore you that you may serve Me; if you utter worthy, not worthless, words, you will be My spokesman" (Jer. 15:19, NIV). Because of his attitude toward God and his calling, Jeremiah was about to forfeit his ministry! In some ways, he was mirroring the words and attitudes of the people of Judah when they questioned God.

The Lord usually balances rebuke with reassurance. He promised once again to make Jeremiah a fortified wall and give him victory over all his enemies (v. 20; see 1:18-19). Jeremiah had to learn to walk by faith, which meant obeying God's Word no matter how he felt, what he saw, or what others might do to him. God never promised Jeremiah an easy job, but He did promise him all that he needed to do his work faithfully.

Is it unusual for chosen servants of God to become discouraged and endanger their own ministries? No, because every servant of God is human and subject to the weaknesses of human nature. Moses became discouraged and wanted to die (Num. 11:10-15); Joshua was ready to quit and leave the Promised Land (Josh. 7:6-11); Elijah even abandoned his place of duty and hoped to die (1 Kings 19); and Jonah became so angry he refused to help the very people he came to save! (Jonah 4) God doesn't want us to ignore our feelings, because that would make us less than human, but He does want us to trust Him to change our feelings and start walking by faith (see 2 Cor. 1:3-11).

3. A message about Jeremiah's strange conduct (Jer. 16:1-21)

In order to get the attention of the people, God sometimes told the prophets to do unusual things. Isaiah gave two of his sons odd names, which he used as a text for a message (Isa. 8), and he also dressed like a prisoner of war to call attention to a coming conflict (Isa. 20). We've already noted the many "action sermons" of both Jeremiah and Ezekiel.

Jeremiah's prohibitions (vv. 1-9). The Lord forbade Jeremiah from participating in three normal and acceptable activities: getting married, mourning for the dead, and attending feasts. All Jewish men were expected to be married by age twenty. In fact, the rabbis pronounced a curse on any who refused to marry and beget children. Certainly Jeremiah would have appreciated having a loving wife to encourage him, but this blessing was not his to enjoy. When you consider all the trials he endured and the enemies he made, Jeremiah was probably better off a single man. But his refusing marriage was a symbolic act, for the sons and daughters in Jewish families would either die by the sword or starve to death in the coming Babylonian invasion. Whenever anybody asked Jeremiah why he wasn't married, he had opportunity to share God's message of the coming judgment.

The Jewish people in Bible times were experts at mourning and marrying, but Jeremiah was forbidden to attend funerals or weddings and the feasts connected with them. What did this unsociable conduct say to the people? For one thing, God had removed His peace and comfort from the nation. Moreover, the judgment that was coming would be so terrible that the people would be unable to express their grief. There would be so many corpses and so few survivors that nobody would bury the dead, let alone comfort whatever family member remained.

As for wedding feasts, how could people celebrate with such a cloud of destruction hovering over the nation? The days would come when the happy voices of brides and bridegrooms would cease. In fact, all joy and gladness would flee from the land. The exiles would form a funeral march and go to Babylon.

Jeremiah's explanation (vv. 10-13, 16-18). It seems strange that the people would ask why the Lord decreed such a terrible judgment for His people. Surely they knew the terms of His covenant and the extent of their own sins, but they were led astray by the false prophets and comfortable in their sins, and their conscience was dead. Their unbiblical theology gave them a false assurance that God would never abandon His people or allow the Gentiles to desecrate the holy city and the temple. How wrong they were!

Jeremiah's explanation was simple: They had repeated the sins of their fathers instead of listening to the Law of the Lord and turning from sin. Furthermore, they had not learned from the past judgments that God had sent. This made them even more guilty than their fathers. Had not Assyria taken the Northern Kingdom of Israel captive because of their idolatry? Had not the previous prophets proclaimed the Word of God and warned the people?

Jeremiah used several images to describe the Captivity. The verb "cast you out" (Jer. 16:13) is used for hurling a spear or sending a storm against a ship (Jonah 1:4). God was violently removing His people so the land could be healed and the nation purified (2 Chron. 36:14-21). Jeremiah also used the metaphors of fishing, hunting, and banking (Jer. 16:16-18). The Babylonians would cast out their nets and catch the Jews (Ezek. 12:13), and not one "fish" would escape. If anybody tried to hide in the hills, the fishermen would become hunters and track them down. Why? Because the nation owed a great debt to the Lord for the way they had treated His Law and His land. Now the "note" was due. "I will repay them double for their wickedness and their sin" (Jer. 16:18, NIV) means that God's judgment would be ample and complete.

Jeremiah's consolation (vv. 14-15). In wrath, God remembers mercy (Hab. 3:2), and Jeremiah gave the people a message of hope: The exiles will one day return to their land. So great will be this deliverance that it will be looked upon as a "second exodus" and far outshine the glory of Israel's exodus from Egypt. Later, Jeremiah would explain that the exiles will be in Babylon for seventy years (Jer. 25), and that a remnant would return to the land, rebuild the temple, and establish the nation (23:3; 31:7-9). They would return as a chastened people who would never again turn to the idols of the Gentile nations.

Jeremiah's affirmation (vv. 19-21). In a burst of faith and prophetic joy, Jeremiah saw not only the gathering of the Jewish remnant but also the coming of the Gentile nations from the ends of the earth to worship the true and living God of Israel. Isaiah had this same vision (Isa. 2:1-5; 11:10-16; 45:14), and so did Zechariah (Zech. 8:20-23). The Gentiles will confess their sin of idolatry and admit that the idols were worthless. Then they will be taught to know the Lord. Meanwhile, it's the task of the church today to spread the message of the Gospel to the ends of the earth so that sinners might abandon their false gods, whatever they may be, and trust in Jesus Christ, the Savior of the world.

4. A message about Judah's sins (Jer. 17:1-27)

President Calvin Coolidge came home from church one Sunday, and his wife asked, "What did the preacher preach about?" "Sin," the President said in his usual concise manner. "What did he say about it?" Mrs. Coolidge further inquired, and the President replied, "He was against it."

Jeremiah was against the sins of his people, six of which he named in this chapter.

Idolatry (vv. 1-4). Instead of giving their devotion and obedience to the true and living God, who had blessed them, the Jews adopted the idols of the nations around them and made these false gods more important than Jehovah. At the high places in the hills, they built altars to various gods and planted obscene symbols of the goddess Asherah. This defiled the land—their rich inheritance from Jehovah, and because of their idolatry, their inheritance would be plundered. They would lose everything, and it would be their own fault.

God's holy Law should have been written on their hearts (Prov. 3:3; 7:3; Deut. 6:6, 11:18; 2 Cor. 3:1-3), but instead their sin was engraved there. We may forget our sins, but our sins never forget us. They're inscribed on our hearts until we ask the Lord for forgiveness, and then He cleanses our hearts and makes them new (1 John 1:9; Heb. 10:15-18).

The Apostle John's final admonition to believers in his first epistle is "Little children, keep yourselves from idols"

(1 John 5:21). There were many false gods in that day (1 Cor. 8:1-5), but there are false gods in our world today, such as money, possessions, fame, "success," power, pleasure, achievement, and many more. Anything that we love and trust more than the true and living God, the God and Father of our Lord Jesus Christ, is an idol and must be torn from our hearts.

Unbelief (vv. 5-10). The leaders of Judah were prone to trust their political allies and lean on the arm of flesh instead of depending on the power of God. To emphasize the difference, Jeremiah contrasted a desert bush with a fruitful tree by the water (see Ps. 1:3-4). Unbelief turns life into a parched wasteland; faith makes it a fruitful orchard. Soon, the Babylonian army would overrun the kingdom of Judah, and the land of milk and honey would become a wasteland.

The heart of every problem is the problem in the heart, and the human heart is deceitful (*Jacob* in the Hebrew) and incurable. We often say, "Well, if I know my own heart," *but we don't know our own hearts.* God does. He searches the heart and mind and knows exactly how to reward each person. If we want to know what our hearts are like, we must read the Word and let the Spirit teach us. The hearts of the Jewish leaders were turned away from the Lord and His truth. Consequently, they made unwise decisions and plunged the nation into ruin.

The Jewish people have a record of unbelief. It was unbelief that kept the people of Israel out of the Promised Land (Num. 13–14). It was unbelief that caused them to worship idols and invite the chastening of God during the time of the Judges. During the time of the kingdom, it was unbelief that kept the leaders from repenting and turning to God for help, and they became entangled in the costly politics involving Assyria, Egypt, and Babylon. Would they ever learn?

Greed (v. 11). During those tumultuous days, the rich exploited the poor and became richer, and the courts did nothing about it. "For from the least of them even unto the greatest of them every one is given to covetousness" (Jer. 6:13). Jeremiah quoted a familiar proverb about the partridge, who is supposed to hatch eggs she didn't lay and have the brood desert her—a picture of wealth deserting the rich people who unjustly acquired it. What good would their wealth be when the judgment fell on the land?

Forsaking the Lord (vv. 12-13). The throne of Judah was stained with sin and clouded by shame, but God's throne was glorious and exalted. The Jews considered the ark of the covenant in the holy of holies to be God's throne (Pss. 80:1; 99:1), but even if the temple were destroyed, God's heavenly throne would endure forever (Isa. 6:1). God had never forsaken His people, but they had forsaken Him. This is why Judah was facing terrible judgment. Instead of being written in the Book of Life, those who forsook God were written in the dust where their names perished with them (Ex. 32:32; Ps. 69:28; Phil. 4:3).

Rejecting God's servant (vv. 14-18). This is the fourth of Jeremiah's personal prayers to God for help, and this time the emphasis is on deliverance from his enemies. The people called him a false prophet and kept asking when his dire predictions would come true. They didn't realize that God's delays were opportunities for the nation to repent and be saved from ruin. Except for one episode of unbelief (Jer. 15:15-21), Jeremiah had not tried to run away from his responsibilities nor had he altered the messages God had given him to deliver. But he needed God's help and protection, and the Lord answered his prayers.

Profaning the Sabbath (vv. 19-27). God had given the Sabbath to the Israelites as a special token of their relationship with Him (see Ex. 16:29; 20:8-11; 31:13-17). It was to be a day of rest for the people, their farm animals, and the land.

The people, however, repeatedly disregarded the Law and treated the Sabbath like any other day. Their sin was evidence that their hearts were devoted to material gain and not to the Lord.

A mechanical obedience to the Sabbath law wasn't what God wanted, but obedience that came from their hearts because they loved and feared the Lord. If this were the case, then they would obey *all* His Law, and God could then bless the people, their kings, and their city. If they continued to disobey the Law and desecrate the Sabbath, however, God would have to punish them by destroying their city and their temple.[10]

Jeremiah faithfully and courageously delivered his sermons to the people; he lifted his supplications to the Lord; he poured out his grief over the sins of the nation; and yet the people only hardened their hearts and stubbornly resisted God's truth.

In an age of unconcern and indecision, Jeremiah was burdened and decisive, and God honored him. Humanly speaking, his ministry was a failure, but from the divine perspective, he was an outstanding success. We need men and women of Jeremiah's caliber serving in the church and the nation today. There's a price to pay, but there's also a crown to win.

SIX

JEREMIAH 18-20

The Prophet, the Potter, and the Policeman

"The clay is not attractive in itself, but when the hands of the potter touch it, and the thought of the potter is brought to bear upon it, and the plan of the potter is worked out in it and through it, then there is a real transformation."

—J. Wilbur Chapman[1]

The prophet, of course, was Jeremiah. We don't know who the potter was, although he played an important part in the drama. The policeman was Pashur, the priest in charge of temple security, whose job it was to keep peace in the temple and punish troublemakers. Since Pashur considered Jeremiah to be a troublemaker, he punished him by making him spend a night in the stocks.

Jeremiah is the chief actor in this three-act drama.

1. Jeremiah, the threatened prophet (Jer. 18:1-23)

These events probably occurred during the reign of Jehoiakim, the king who burned Jeremiah's prophetic scrolls

(36:21ff). Unlike his father King Josiah, Jehoiakim had no love for either the Lord or His prophet. He wasn't the least bit interested in what Jeremiah had to say about things political or spiritual.

The sovereignty of God (vv. 1-17). Over thirty words in the Hebrew vocabulary relate directly to pottery, because the manufacture of pottery was a major industry in the Near East in that day. No doubt Jeremiah had passed the potter's house many times, but this time God had a special message for him that, after he preached it, would put him in jail. When you follow the Lord, you never know what will happen to you next.

"He did not get his flash of insight while he was praying, but while he was watching a potter engaged in his daily work," wrote Charles E. Jefferson. "God reveals Himself in strange places and at unexpected seasons. For instance He once revealed Himself in a stable."[2]

The potter sat before two parallel stone wheels that were joined by a shaft. He turned the bottom wheel with his feet and worked the clay on the top wheel as the wheel turned. As Jeremiah watched, he saw that the clay resisted the potter's hand so that the vessel was ruined,[3] but the potter patiently kneaded the clay and made another vessel.

The *interpretation* of the image was national, relating to the house of Israel (vv. 6-10), but the *application* was individual (vv. 11-17), calling for a response from the people of Judah and Jerusalem. It also calls for a personal response from us today.

INTERPRETATION (vv. 5-10). As the potter has power over the clay, so God has sovereign authority over the nations.[4] This doesn't mean that God is irresponsible and arbitrary in what He does, even though He is free to act as He pleases. His actions are always consistent with His nature, which is holy, just, wise, and loving. God doesn't need any advice from us, nor do we have the right to criticize what He does. "For who has known the mind of the Lord? Or who has become His counselor?" (Rom. 11:34, NKJV, quoted from Isa. 40:13 and Jer. 23:18) "But indeed, O man, who are you to reply against God? Will the thing formed say to him who formed it, 'Why have you made me like this?' " (Rom. 9:20, NKJV)

The Lord presented two scenarios that illustrated His sovereign power over nations (Jer. 18:7-10). If He threatened to *judge* a nation and that nation repented, then He would relent and not send the judgment. He did this with Nineveh when Jonah's preaching brought the city to repentance (Jonah 3). On the other hand, if He promised to *bless* a nation, as He did Israel in His covenants, and that nation did evil in His sight, then He could withhold the blessing and send judgment instead. God neither changes in character nor needs to repent of His actions (Mal. 3:6; Num. 23:19), but He has the sovereign freedom to alter His actions depending on the responses of the people.

To be sure, there's mystery involved in the relationship between divine sovereignty and human responsibility, but we don't have to explain the will of God before we can obey it. We live by divine promises and precepts, not theological explanations, and God isn't obligated to explain anything to us. (If He did, we probably wouldn't be able to grasp it!) "The secret things belong to the Lord our God, but those things which are revealed belong to us and to our children forever, that we may do all the words of this Law" (Deut. 29:29, NKJV). Jesus promised that if we obey what we know, God will reveal more of His truth to us (John 7:17).

APPLICATION (JER. 18:11-17). Nations are made up of individuals, and individuals have the ability to receive God's Word or reject it. Yes, humans are made from the dust (Gen. 2:7) and live in a fragile body (Job 4:19; 10:9; 2 Cor. 4:7). Unlike the clay on the potter's wheel, however, we have the ability to resist. God uses many different hands to mold our lives—parents, siblings, teachers, ministers, authors—and we can fight against them. But if we do, we're fighting against God.

God announced that He was "framing" evil ("preparing," NIV; "fashioning," NASB; a word related to "potter" in the Hebrew) against the kingdom of Judah. If the people would repent, however, He would deliver them. But the people were so chained to their sins that they chose to follow their own evil plans. They would rather worship dead idols and suffer for it than serve the true and living God and enjoy His blessings! Truly, the heart is deceitful and desperately wicked! (Jer. 17:9)

In rejecting their God and choosing dumb idols, the people of Judah were acting contrary to everything reasonable. God made them for Himself, and they could not succeed apart from Him. The birds obey what God tells them to do (8:7); even the heathen nations don't abandon their gods, false as these gods are. Water in nature is consistent: On the heights, it becomes snow; at lower levels, it flows in the streams. God's people, however, were totally inconsistent, willing to enjoy God's blessings but not willing to obey the laws of God that governed those blessings. If nature acted like that, where would we be?

Instead of walking on God's clear and safe highway of holiness (Isa. 35:8), the people were on a dangerous and painful detour because they abandoned the ancient paths of God's holy Law. Because they wouldn't repent, God had to chasten them; this meant ruin for the land and exile for the people. Instead of His face shining upon them in blessing (Num. 6:24-26), God would turn His back to them and leave them to their own devices.

Like the patient potter, God is willing to "mold us again" when we resist Him and damage our own lives. The famous

Scottish preacher Alexander Whyte used to say that the victorious Christian life was "a series of new beginnings." No failure in our lives need be fatal or final, although we certainly suffer for our sins. God gave new beginnings to Abraham, Moses, David, Jonah, and Peter when they failed, and He can do the same for us today.

The conspiracy of the enemy (v. 18). Proud sinners don't enjoy hearing about God's sovereignty or the threat of impending judgment. They think that by silencing the messenger they will silence the Lord. "He who sits in the heavens shall laugh; the Lord shall have them in derision" (Ps. 2:4, NKJV). Their argument was "We have plenty of priests, prophets, and elders, so we can do without Jeremiah!"

This wasn't the first time Jeremiah had faced a conspiracy that threatened his ministry and his life (Jer. 11:18-23; 12:6; 15:15), and it wouldn't be the last time. His enemies plotted a "smear campaign" consisting of lies about him (see 9:3). The plot probably included quotations from his messages that suggested he was a traitor to the kingdom of Judah. Like the men who plotted against Jesus, Jeremiah's enemies tried to prove he was breaking the law and stirring up the people (Luke 23:1-7).

Faithful servants of God don't enjoy opposition, but they learn to expect it. "In the world you will have tribulation," promised Jesus, "but be of good cheer, I have overcome the world" (John 16:33, NKJV). He also said, "If the world hates you, you know that it hated Me before it hated you" (15:18). And Paul reminded Timothy and us, "Yes, and all who desire to live godly in Christ Jesus will suffer persecution" (2 Tim. 3:12, NKJV).

The agony of the prophet (vv. 19-23). This is the fifth of Jeremiah's private "laments" to the Lord concerning his situation and his ministry (see Jer. 11:18-23; 12:1-5; 15:10-18; 17:14-18; 20:7-18). His words seem terribly harsh to us and unlike the spirit of Jesus, but keep in mind that Jeremiah was a divinely appointed prophet who represented God to the nation. Those who opposed him were opposing God, and Jeremiah asked God to deal with them (Deut. 32:35; see Rom. 12:17-19).

Like Elijah and all the other prophets, Jeremiah was "a man subject to like passions as we are" (James 5:17, "with a nature like ours," NKJV), and he felt deep pain because the leaders rejected the truth. I suppose if you and I were attacked by hateful enemies who lied about us, set traps for us, and dug pits for us, we'd get upset and ask God to deal with them. At least Jeremiah expressed himself honestly to God and left the matter with Him. He needed to remember God's promises when He called him (Jer. 1:7-10, 17-19) and rest in the assurance that the Lord would see him through.

There is a righteous anger against sin that is acceptable to God. "Be angry, and do not sin" (Eph. 4:26, NKJV, quoted from Ps. 4:4). "You who love the Lord, hate evil!" (Ps. 97:10, NKJV; see Rom. 12:9) Jesus was angry at the hardening of the hearts of His critics (Mark 3:5), and Paul was angry because of professed believers who were leading others astray. "Who is led into sin and I do not inwardly burn?" (2 Cor. 11:29, NIV) Unrighteous anger takes matters into its own hands and seeks to destroy the offender, while righteous anger turns the matter over to God and seeks to help the offended. Anguish is anger plus love, and it isn't easy to maintain a holy balance. If Jeremiah seems too angry to us, perhaps some of us today aren't angry enough at the evil in this world. Thanks to the media, we're exposed to so much violence and sin that we tend to accept it as a normal part of life and want to do nothing about it. Crusading has given way to compromising, and it isn't "politically correct" to be dogmatic or critical of ideas that are definitely unbiblical.

2. Jeremiah, the persecuted prophet (Jer. 19:1–20:6)
The theme of the potter continues with another "action sermon" from Jeremiah, a sermon that cost him a beating and a night in the stocks.

Jeremiah preaches the sermon (vv. 1-9). At the command of the Lord, Jeremiah made a second trip to the potter's house, this time as a customer and not a spectator, and he took with him some of the Jewish elders. Knowing their evil plots against him, it's an evidence of his faith that he was willing to walk with them and then do so daring a thing as declare *in their very presence* that disaster was coming to the land because of their sins. Obviously his prayer to the Lord had brought him peace and courage.

The east gate was the Potsherd Gate, where the potters worked and the broken pottery was thrown. It overlooked the Valley of the Son of Hinnom, the Jerusalem garbage dump (Gehenna). But Jeremiah turned the gate into a pulpit and declared impending disaster because of what the kings of Judah had done: forsaken God, worshiped idols, desecrated the temple, murdered the innocent, and offered their children in altar fires dedicated to Baal.

This valley had been a center for idol worship, but Josiah had desecrated it by making it a garbage dump. *Topheth* means "a fire pit, a hearth," because the little children had been put through the fires there. After the Babylonian invasion, however, the new name would be "The Valley of Slaughter." The siege would be so bad that the Jews would have to eat their own children to stay alive!

Jeremiah announces judgment (vv. 10-15). "I will make void[5] the counsel of Judah and Jerusalem in this place" (19:7). To demonstrate this, Jeremiah broke a clay jar and said, "This is what the Lord Almighty says: 'I will smash this nation and this city just as this potter's jar is smashed and cannot be repaired'" (v. 11, NIV). The nation was beyond discipline

(2:23), beyond prayer (7:16), and now, beyond repair! They had so hardened themselves against the Lord that all hope was gone.

In the Near East in that day, kings and generals often smashed clay jars in a special ceremony before they went out to battle, symbolic of their total defeat of their enemies. This image is also used of the Messiah in Psalm 2:9: "You shall break them [the enemy nations] with a rod of iron; You shall dash them in pieces like a potter's vessel" (NKJV). But here it was God smashing His own people!

We can only imagine how angry the elders were who had accompanied Jeremiah to the Potsherd Gate. After all, they and the priests (and Jeremiah was a priest) had endorsed the "peace messages" of the false prophets as well as the political schemes of the civil leaders who hoped to get help from Judah's ungodly allies. But what Jeremiah did next made them even more angry, because *he went to the temple and preached the sermon again!* For a man who was broken before God, he certainly had courage before his enemies, but he was trusting God's promise of help (Jer. 1:7-10, 17-19), and the Lord was sustaining him.

Can nations and individuals sin so greatly that even God can't restore them? Yes, they can. As long as the clay is pliable in the hands of the potter, he can make it again if it's marred (18:4), but when the clay becomes hard, it's too late to re-form it. *Judgment is the only response to willful apostasy.* The Northern Kingdom of Israel refused to repent, and the Assyrians took it captive. Now the Southern Kingdom of Judah was resisting God's truth, and Babylon would destroy the land and deport the people. The Jewish people rejected their King when they asked Pilate to crucify Jesus; forty years later, the Romans did to Jerusalem what the Babylonians had done six centuries before. "There is a sin unto death" (1 John 5:16).

Jeremiah experiences pain (20:1-6). What before had been threats now became a reality. Pashur, son of Immer,[6] assistant to the high priest and chief security officer for the temple, didn't like what Jeremiah was saying. Therefore, he had Jeremiah arrested, beaten, and put into the stocks until the next day. The stocks were located at a prominent place in the temple area, in order to add shame to pain. Spending all night with your body bent and twisted wouldn't be at all comfortable, and when you add the pain of the beating, you can imagine how Jeremiah felt.

Being beaten and put into the stocks was the first of several acts of persecution the leaders inflicted on Jeremiah. They threatened to kill him (Jer. 26), they accused him falsely and imprisoned him (37:11-21), and they put him into a pit (38:1-13). He was an official prisoner until Nebuchadnezzar set him free (39:11-18).

God, however, met with Jeremiah that night (see Acts 18:9-11; 23:11; 27:23-24) and gave him a special message and a new name for Pashur: Magor-Missabib, which means "terror on every side" (NIV). Jeremiah had used this phrase before (Jer. 6:25) and would use it again (46:5; 49:5, 29). It described what would happen to Jerusalem when the Babylonian army finally moved in.

For the first time, Jeremiah named the king of Babylon as the invader (20:4).[7] Previously, Jeremiah had announced an invasion from "the North" (see 1:13-15; 3:12, 18; 4:5-9; 6:1, 22-26; 10:22), but he hadn't named the invading nation. Now the tool of God's discipline was identified as Babylon, and Jeremiah would mention Babylon in one way or another 200 times in his book.

Pashur's treatment of Jeremiah would receive just recompense, for he and his family would be taken captive to Babylon, and there they would die. For a Jew to be buried outside his own land was considered a judgment, for the Gentile lands were considered unclean. For Pashur and his friends, however, what difference would that make? They'd been preaching lies in the name of the God of truth and had been encouraging idolatry in the temple of the holy God. So why not live in a land of lies and idols and eventually be buried there? They'd be right at home!

If the events described in Jeremiah 18–20 took place during the reign of Jehoiakim (607–597 B.C.), then it didn't take long for Jeremiah's prophecy to be fulfilled. In 605, Nebuchadnezzar plundered the temple and took Jehoiakim and the nobles to Babylon. In 597, he carried off over 10,000 people, and eleven years later, he burned the temple and the city and left it in ruins. Five years later, he deported another group of exiles.

3. Jeremiah, the discouraged prophet (Jer. 20:7-18)

This is the last of Jeremiah's recorded laments; it's a human blending of grief and joy, prayer and despair, praise and perplexity. When you call to mind the sensitive nature of this man, you aren't surprised that he's on the mountaintop one minute and in the deepest valley the next. Jeremiah, however, lived above his moods and did the will of God regardless of how he felt. In this honest expression of his deepest emotions, the prophet dealt with three important concerns: God's call (vv. 7-9), his daily peril (vv. 10-13), and his inner despair (vv. 14-18).

His "deceptive" call (vv. 7-9). When the servants of God find themselves in trouble because they've been faithful in ministry, they're often tempted to question their call and reconsider their vocation. Then what do they do? One of the first things they ought to do is *talk to the Lord about it and tell Him the truth.*

The word translated "deceived" carries with it the idea of being enticed or seduced. Of course, God doesn't lie (Titus

1:2), but Jeremiah felt that the Lord had taken advantage of him and lured him into the ministry. "You overpowered me and prevailed" (Jer. 20:7, NIV). Jeremiah felt like a helpless maiden who had been seduced then taken advantage of by a deceptive "lover." This is strong language, but at least Jeremiah said it privately to God and not publicly to others.

When you review the account of Jeremiah's call (Jer. 1), you find no evidence that God had enticed him. The Lord had told him plainly that he would have a difficult time. If he trusted the Lord, however, He would make him a fortified city and a bronze wall before his enemies. God had warned His servant that the demands of ministry would increase and he'd have to grow in order to keep going (12:5). What Jeremiah's ministry was doing for the nation was important, but even more important was what Jeremiah's ministry was doing *for Jeremiah.* As we serve the Lord, our capacity for ministry should increase and enable us to do much more than we ever thought we could do.

After you've told God how you feel, what do you do next? Jeremiah resolved to quit being a prophet! He decided to keep his mouth shut and not even mention the Lord to anybody. But that didn't work, because the message of God was like a burning in his heart and a fire in his bones (see Luke 24:32). Jeremiah didn't preach because he had to say something but because he had something to say, and not saying it would have destroyed him. Paul had the same attitude: "Yet when I preach the Gospel, I cannot boast, for I am compelled to preach. Woe to me if I do not preach the Gospel!" (1 Cor. 9:16, NIV)

His daily peril (vv. 10-13). Having settled the matter of his call, Jeremiah then looked away from himself to the enemies around him. Faith doesn't ignore problems; it faces them honestly and seeks God's help in solving them. No matter how much he was constrained to preach God's Word, Jeremiah had to deal with the fact that many people wanted him to keep quiet and would take the necessary steps to silence him.

Borrowing the new name God gave Pashur (Jer. 20:3), it's possible that Jeremiah's enemies used "Terror on every side" as a nickname for the prophet. It was another way to ridicule his prophecies before the people. They watched him and took note of what he did and said so they could find something criminal to report to the authorities. David had a similar experience (Ps. 31:13), and this is the way our Lord's enemies treated Him (Matt. 22:15ff).

Jeremiah's mood swings from expressing courage to seeking revenge and then to rejoicing in worship (Jer. 20:11-13). Remembering the promises God gave him at his call, Jeremiah was confident that the Lord was with him and would deal effectively with his enemies. Instead of dishonoring him, his enemies would themselves be dishonored. Since his words in verse 12 are almost identical to his prayer in 11:20, perhaps it's one he prayed often.

His deep despair (vv. 14-18). Having committed his cause to the Lord, Jeremiah had every reason to sing, for now the Lord would have to bear his burdens and help fight his battles. "Trust in Him at all times, you people; pour out your heart before Him, God is a refuge for us" (Ps. 62:8, NKJV).

Jeremiah's euphoria didn't last long, however, because in the next breath he was cursing his birthday (Jer. 15:10; see Job 3). Jewish parents would rejoice at the birth of a son who could wear the family name and be able to sustain his parents in their old age. A priestly family like Jeremiah's would be especially grateful for a son who could carry on the ministry to the Lord.

But Jeremiah's ideas were different. The messenger who announced that a son had been born would bring joy to the family and expect a reward for bringing such good news, but

Jeremiah asked that the messenger be treated like Sodom and Gomorrah! He wanted that man to awaken to weeping in the morning and to hear battle cries every noon! "Why didn't my mother's womb become my tomb?" asked the prophet. "My life is nothing but trouble and sorrow and shame! Better that I had never lived!"

"Why came I forth out of the womb?" is an easy question to answer: because God had a special purpose for your life and designed you to fulfill it (Jer. 1:4-5; Ps. 139:13-16). God makes no mistakes when He calls His servants, and we should take care not to question His wisdom. All of us have had times of discouragement when we've felt like quitting, but that's when we must look beyond our feelings and circumstances and see the greatness and wisdom of God.

As V. Raymond Edman, former president of Wheaton College (Ill.), often said to the students, "It's always too soon to quit."

And it is!

SEVEN

JEREMIAH 21–24

Kings on Parade

"The tumult and the shouting dies–
The captains and the kings depart–
Still stands Thine ancient Sacrifice
An humble and a contrite heart.
Lord God of Hosts, be with us yet,
Lest we forget–lest we forget!"
–Rudyard Kipling, "Recessional"

Kipling's "Recessional" was published in 1897 when Queen Victoria's diamond jubilee was celebrated in Great Britain. The poem was a quiet warning to the British people to beware of overconfidence in their hour of imperial glory. Perhaps Kipling had the words of Daniel in mind: "The Most High rules in the kingdom of men, and gives it to whomever He chooses" (Dan. 4:25, NKJV), or he may have been thinking of Proverbs 16:18: "Pride goes before destruction, and a haughty spirit before a fall" (NKJV).

Jeremiah wrote a more pointed "Recessional" for the kingdom of Judah as he described one king after another leaving the scene and marching off to shameful judgment. In the great days of David, Hezekiah, and Josiah, the nation had honored the Lord, but now Judah was rapidly moving toward defeat and disgrace. In these pivotal chapters, Jeremiah delivered four important messages to the leaders and to the people.

1. God opposes the leaders of Judah (Jer. 21:1-14)

These events probably took place in the year 588 when the invincible Babylonian army was camped around the walls of Jerusalem. Hoping to secure help from Egypt, weak King Zedekiah had rebelled against Nebuchadnezzar by refusing to pay tribute (2 Chron. 36:13; see Ezek. 17:11-18); now Judah was suffering the dreadful consequences of his foolish decision. In desperation, he looked to Jeremiah for help by sending Zephaniah the priest and Pashur, one of the court officers, to see whether the prophet could get guidance from the Lord.[1] The king hoped that Jehovah would send a miraculous deliverance to Jerusalem as He had done in the days of godly King Hezekiah (2 Kings 18–19). Jeremiah, however, responded with dire pronouncements to the king (Jer. 21:3-7), the people (vv. 8-10), and the house of David (vv. 11-14).

A pronouncement to King Zedekiah (vv. 3-7). Not only would God refuse to deliver the city from the enemy, but also He would fight *with* the enemy and bring about Jerusalem's defeat! Judah's military might would be ineffective against the Chaldean army. Whereas in the past, God's mighty "outstretched arm" and "strong hand" had worked *for* His people (Deut. 4:34; 5:15; 26:8), now He would work *against* them, because the nation had turned against God. "To the faithful You show Yourself faithful . . . but to the crooked You show Yourself shrewd" (Ps. 18:25-26, NIV).

It seems strange that the Lord would use words like "anger," "fury," and "great wrath" (Jer. 21:5) to describe His disposition toward His own people. Yet these words were a part of His covenant with the people, and the nation knew the terms of the covenant (see Deut. 29:23, 28; 32:16-17, 21, 29; Lev. 26:27-28). God had warned the Jews repeatedly that their disobedience would arouse His anger and force Him to bring judgment to the land, but the leaders wouldn't listen. They preferred dead idols to the living God, and power politics to simple faith in His Word.

Jeremiah announced that the people in Jerusalem would die of famine, pestilence, or the sword; many of the survivors would even be taken captive to Babylon. King Zedekiah and his officers would be handed over to Nebuchadnezzar and judged. That's exactly what happened. The siege began January 15, 588, and ended July 18, 586, a period of just over thirty months.[2] After Zedekiah, his sons, and his nobles were captured, his sons were slain before the eyes of the king, who was then blinded and taken to Babylon, where he died (Jer. 39:1-10; 52:8-11, 24-27; 2 Kings 25).

A pronouncement to the people (vv. 8-10). There was no hope for the king, but the Lord did offer hope to the people if they would surrender to Nebuchadnezzar (see Jer. 38:17-23). God set before them two ways—the way of life and the way of death—a choice that must have reminded them of the words of the covenant (Deut. 11:26-32; 30:15-20; see Jer. 27:12-13; 38:2-3, 17-18). With God, we must decide one way or the other (Ps. 1); it's not possible to be neutral (Matt. 7:13-29; 12:22-30).

Of course, to surrender to the enemy was an act of treason, and Jeremiah eventually got into trouble for advocating this plan (Jer. 37:11-21; 38:1-6). The phrase "his life shall be unto him for a prey" (21:9) is literally "his life shall be to him as plunder" (see 38:2; 39:18; 45:5). The Babylonians would treat the deserters like spoils of war, and the Jews, after losing everything in the siege, would be happy to escape with their lives.

Since Nebuchadnezzar was doing the work of God in punishing the kingdom of Judah (50:9, 23; 51:20), and since God was allied with Babylon in fighting Judah, to surrender to Babylon really meant to surrender to the will of God. It meant to confess guilt and submit to the hand of the Lord. Rebellion against the Babylonians was rebellion against the Lord, and that was the way of death.

As God's people today, we need to realize that the only safe and sane response to God's chastening hand is *submission.* "Furthermore, we have had human fathers who corrected us, and we paid them respect. Shall we not much more readily be in subjection to the Father of spirits and live?" (Heb. 12:9, NKJV) The implication of the question is that we might not live if we don't submit to the will of God! "There is a sin not unto death" (1 John 5:17).

A pronouncement to the house of David (vv. 11-14). Here the Lord spoke to David's dynasty—the kings who sat on the throne because of God's covenant with David (2 Sam. 7). If they obeyed God's Law and executed justice in the land, God would keep His promise and maintain David's royal dynasty. If they disobeyed, however, the kings would lose their throne rights. Once again, God was simply reminding them of the terms of the covenant and urging them to obey His Word.[3]

The people of Jerusalem were certain that their city was impregnable and that there was no need to be afraid. Surrounded on three sides by valleys—Hinnom on the south and west, and Kidron on the east—the city had to defend itself only on the north. Jerusalem's inhabitants saw themselves "enthroned" on the rocky plateau, but God would soon dethrone them and cause them to lose their crown. Since the Babylonian army did set fire to the city, God did "kindle a fire in the forest" (Jer. 21:14). The phrase "the forest" probably refers to the structures in the city, especially to the king's palace, "the house of the forest of Lebanon" (1 Kings 7:2;

10:17, 21). The cedars of Lebanon were used to construct various buildings in the city.

This chapter begins with a king's cry for help and ends with a prophet's pronouncement of doom. What a tragedy!

2. God discloses the fate of the kings (Jer. 22:1–23:8)
Godly King Josiah reigned for thirty-one years and sought to lead the people back to God. But the last four kings of Judah were wicked men, even though three of them were Josiah's sons and one was his grandson (Jehoiachin).

Jehoahaz, or Shallum, succeeded Josiah and reigned only three months (Jer. 22:10-12; 2 Kings 23:30-33). Pharaoh Necho deported him to Egypt, where he died.

Jehoiakim, also called Eliakim, reigned for eleven years (Jer. 22:13-23; 2 Kings 23:34–24:6) and died in Jerusalem. He was followed by his son *Jehoiachin,* also called Jeconiah and Coniah, whose reign lasted only three months (Jer. 22:24-30; 2 Kings 24:6-12). Nebuchadnezzar took him to Babylon, where eventually he died.

The last king of Judah was *Zedekiah* who reigned eleven years and saw the kingdom and the holy city destroyed by Babylon (Jer. 22:1-9; 2 Kings 24:17–25:21). He was blinded and taken to Babylon to die. As Kipling wrote, "The captains and the kings depart."

Jeremiah disclosed the truth about those four kings, but then he made a promise about Messiah—the Righteous Branch (King) who would one day reign and execute justice in the land.

Zedekiah—callousness (22:1-9). The king had sent messengers to Jeremiah, but the prophet went *personally* to the palace to deliver God's message. Zedekiah was sitting on David's throne, in David's house of cedar (2 Sam. 5:11; 7:2, 7), benefiting from the covenant God had made with David (2 Sam. 7), and yet the king wasn't serving the Lord as David had served Him. Jeremiah repeated what he had preached before (Jer. 21:12), that it was time for the king and his nobles to obey God's Law and execute justice in the land. They were exploiting the poor and needy, shedding innocent blood, and refusing to repent and turn to God.

In 2 Samuel 7, there is a dual meaning to the word "house": a literal building (the temple David wanted to construct for God) and the royal house (dynasty) God established through David by His gracious covenant. These same two meanings are woven into Jeremiah's message: God will destroy both the royal palace and the Davidic dynasty because of the sins of the kings. The royal house of cedar would be cut down and burned as the Chaldean soldiers went through the city like men chopping down a forest in Lebanon.

Meanwhile, Jeremiah appeared to be giving the leaders a small window of opportunity: If they would repent and do justice, God would deliver the city and establish David's throne (Jer. 22:4). Their hearts, however, were hard, and they would not listen. The ruins of Jerusalem would be a monument to their wickedness.

Jehoahaz (Shallum)—hopelessness (22:10-12). The death of godly King Josiah a decade before had brought great sorrow to the people. Even Jeremiah had written a lamentation honoring the dead monarch (2 Chron. 35:25). But there was no hope for the nation in looking back and weeping over a dead past. Nor was there hope in trusting that King Jehoahaz (Shallum) would be released from Egypt, where he was prisoner of Pharaoh Necho (2 Chron. 36:1-4). Apparently there was a pro-Jehoahaz party in Judah that pinned their hopes on his return, and perhaps some of the false prophets encouraged this expectation. Jeremiah, however, announced that Jehoahaz would never return to Judah but would die in Egypt.

Instead of looking to a dead past or trusting in a deposed

leader, the people should have been dealing with the issues of that hour and looking to the Lord for His help. Josiah was dead; Jehoahaz was exiled; it was time for Zedekiah to follow the example of his godly father Josiah and lead the people back to the worship of the true God.

Jehoiakim (Eliakim)—covetousness (22:13-23).[4] During a time of international crisis, Jehoiakim was more concerned about building his own spacious palace than he was building a righteous kingdom, and he even used unpaid Jewish slave labor to do it! It was against the law to hold back wages or to enslave fellow Jews (Ex. 21:1-11; Lev. 15:12-23; 19:13; Deut. 24:14-15; James 5:1-6). The nation was decaying and dying while the king was admiring his palace, the spacious rooms, the large windows, and the decorated cedar paneled walls. Jehoiakim wasn't much different from some modern politicians who profit from dishonest gain while they ignore the cries of the poor and needy.

"Does it make you a king to have more and more cedar?" (Jer. 22:15, NIV) asked the prophet. Then he reminded him that his father King Josiah lived comfortably and still did what was just and right. Josiah defended the cause of the poor, and God blessed him, but Jehoiakim thought only of himself. It didn't worry him that God watched as he robbed the poor, killed the innocent, and oppressed the just in order to satisfy his craving for luxury.

Jeremiah moved from "him" (third person) in verse 13 to "you" (second person) in verse 15, and then he named the king in verse 18. He announced that the king's burial would be quite unlike that given to his beloved father. The nation mourned Josiah's untimely death, but the Jews wouldn't weep when Jehoiakim died, nor would they bury him like a king. Who would pay for an expensive funeral just to bury a donkey? The carcass would be thrown on the garbage dump, where the scavengers and vermin would devour it (Jer.

36:30). Even Jehoiakim's end would be in fulfillment of the covenant curses (Deut. 28:26).[5]

Before going on to discuss the next king, Jeremiah paused to address the people of Jerusalem and describe their terrible plight (Jer. 22:20-23). The advance of the Chaldean army had crushed their allies ("lovers"), who also would be sent into exile. Like the desert wind, the Babylonian soldiers would "round up" Judah's evil leaders and sweep them away. The king and his nobles, living carelessly in the cedar palace ("Lebanon"), would soon suffer terrible pain like a woman in travail. The Lord had warned them, but they felt so secure that they wouldn't listen. The peace promised by the false prophets would never materialize. For the city of Jerusalem, it was the end.

Jehoiachin (Coniah, Jeconiah)—childlessness (22:24-30). The son of Jehoiakim, he reigned only three months and ten days before he was deported with the queen mother to Babylon and replaced by his uncle, Zedekiah (2 Chron. 36:9-10; 2 Kings 24:8-17). Jehoiachin was a wicked man, and Jeremiah 22:26 suggests that his mother was as much to blame as his ungodly father. Jeremiah had warned both the king and the queen mother, but they wouldn't listen (13:18-19).

If the king were the very signet ring on God's right hand, God would casually take it off and hand it to the Babylonians (22:24-27). The signet ring was valuable because it was used to prove authority, identify possessions, and "sign" official documents, but Jehoiachin was useless to the Lord, fit only to be thrown away in Babylon.[6]

The question in verse 28 is constructed in such a way that "no" is the answer expected. The people of Judah didn't consider Jehoiachin a broken pot to be tossed away on the trash heap. In fact, one of the false prophets predicted that Jehoiachin would return to Judah, deliver the nation, and reign once again in power (28:1-4). God, however, had another plan for this evil man and his family; the king, his mother, and his sons were all deported to Babylon, where they died.

Jehoiachin had at least seven children (1 Chron. 3:17-18) by several wives (2 Kings 24:15), but none of them would sit on the throne of David. God declared that He would treat Jehoiachin as if the man were childless. Zedekiah, the last king of Judah, saw the Babylonians slay his sons, and it's likely that he himself died before Jehoiachin was freed from prison (Jer. 52:10-11, 31-34). This means that Jehoiachin was the last surviving king in David's line.

Of course, Jesus Christ is the "son of David" (Matt. 1:1; Rom. 1:3) and one day will restore the fortunes of Israel and reign from David's throne (Luke 1:30-33, 67-79). The genealogy in Matthew 1 traces Christ's ancestry through His legal father Joseph. Since Jehoiachin is in that family tree (Matt. 1:11), however, none of his descendants can claim the throne because of the curse pronounced in Jeremiah 22:24-30. Our Lord gets His Davidic throne rights through His mother Mary, whose genealogy is given in Luke 3:21-38. From Abraham to David, the lists are similar, but from David on, they differ. Luke traced the line through David's son Nathan and thus avoided Jehoiachin, a descendant of Solomon. Jesus Christ has every right to David's throne, and His future reign is what Jeremiah dealt with in the next section.

Messiah the King—righteousness (23:1-8). Jeremiah denounced *all* the leaders ("shepherds") of Judah for the ruthless way they treated the helpless people (vv. 1-4). Instead of *leading* the flock in love, they *drove* it mercilessly and exploited it. The shepherds didn't visit ("care for") the sheep, but God would visit the leaders with punishment. Because the leaders disobeyed the Law and refused to trust God, they destroyed the nation and scattered the flock among the Gentiles. God, however, promised to regather His people and transform the remnant into a nation. (The word "remnant" is used nineteen times in Jeremiah.) A remnant did return to Judah after the Captivity, rebuild the temple, and restore national life.

Jeremiah, however, promised a much greater regathering of the Jews—a greater miracle than their deliverance from Egypt (vv. 7-8; see 16:14-15). God will call His people from the nations of the world, gather them in their land, purge them, and then send them their promised Messiah (Jer. 30; Isa. 2:1-5; 4:1-6; 9:1-7; 11:1–12:6; Zech. 12–14). David's "family tree" might have been cut down, but a "branch" (shoot) would grow from the stump and become Ruler of the nation (Isa. 11:1; 53:2).

In contrast to the unrighteous kings Jeremiah had been describing, this King will be righteous and rule justly. The kingdoms of Israel (northern) and Judah (southern) will be united into one nation; they will experience salvation and they will live in peace and safety. The name of this King is "Jehovah Tsidkenu—The Lord our Righteousness" (see Jer. 33:15-16). According to 1 Corinthians 1:30 and 2 Corinthians 5:21, this exalted name applies only to Jesus Christ. When you put your faith in Jesus Christ, His righteousness is put into your account and you are declared righteous before God. This is called "being justified by faith" (Rom. 3:21–5:11).

No matter how dark the day may be, God sends the light of hope through His promises. The godly remnant in Judah must have been encouraged when they heard Jeremiah's words, and the promises must have sustained them during the difficult days of the Captivity. The return of the Jews to their land after the Captivity was but a foreshadowing of the great worldwide regathering that will occur in the last days when "He shall send His angels with a great sound of a trumpet, and they shall gather together His elect from the four winds, from one end of heaven to the other" (Matt. 24:31).

3. God exposes the sins of the false prophets (Jer. 23:9-40)

What God said, as recorded in Jeremiah 14:14, summarizes this entire section: "The prophets prophesy lies in My name. I have not sent them, commanded them, nor spoken to them; they prophesy to you a false vision, divination, a worthless thing, and the deceit of their heart" (NKJV). Jeremiah focused on three areas in their lives that were especially abhorrent.

Their disgraceful conduct (vv. 9-15). True prophets know how serious it is to be called by God to declare His Word, and they accept the responsibility with fear and trembling. When they see self-styled prophets living like sinners, it grieves them. No wonder Jeremiah had a broken heart and trembled like a drunken man! He realized what the false prophets were doing to the people and the land, and it made him sick. "Horror [indignation][7] hath taken hold upon me because of the wicked that forsake Thy Law" (Ps. 119:53).

The false prophets were committing adultery and thronging the houses of prostitution (Jer. 5:7). Then they would go to the temple and pretend to worship Jehovah (23:11), turning God's house into a den of thieves (7:9-11). But the word "adultery" also includes their worship of idols, turning from the true God (to whom Israel was "married") and being unfaithful to their covenant promises.

The false prophets had led the Northern Kingdom of Israel astray (23:13), and now they were leading the Southern Kingdom of Judah astray (v. 14). Baal was the Canaanite rain god to whom the Jews were prone to turn for help in times of drought (1 Kings 17–18), and his worship included "sacred prostitution." Jerusalem was becoming like Sodom and Gomorrah—cities so wicked God had to destroy them (Jer. 20:16; Gen. 18–19).

The land was suffering a severe drought (Jer. 23:10; see chap. 14) because the false prophets led the people to violate the terms of their covenant with God. The Lord promised to send the early and latter rains if they obeyed Him (Deut. 11:10-15; 28:12), but He also warned them that He would make the heavens brass and the earth iron if they disobeyed Him (11:16-17; 28:23-24). "Because of the curse the land lies parched" (Jer. 23:10, NIV). But the sinners refused to escape, even though God had promised to judge them in due time (vv. 12, 15).

Whenever a nation needs healing, it's usually because God's people aren't obeying and serving Him as they should. We like to blame dishonest politicians and various purveyors of pleasure for a nation's decline in morality, but God blames *His own people.* "If My people, which are called by My name, shall humble themselves, and pray, and seek My face, and turn from their wicked ways, then will I hear from heaven, and will forgive their sin, and will heal their land" (2 Chron. 7:14).

Their dishonest message (vv. 16-32). To begin with, the false prophets offered the people *a false hope (Jer. 23:16-20).* "The Lord says: You will have peace. . . . No harm will come to you" (v. 17, NIV; see 6:13-15; 8:10-12). Of course, this was a popular message, and the frightened people grabbed it and held on to it. But the false prophets hadn't heard that message in God's council; they made it up out of their own hearts. Instead of peace, a storm was brewing from the Lord (23:20). God was about to vent His holy anger on His sinful people, and when they finally understood His purposes, it would be too late to stop the whirlwind.

Not only did the false prophets give the people a false hope, but they also ministered under *a false authority* (23:21-24). God hadn't spoken to them, yet they prophesied. God hadn't called them, yet they ran with their message. If they were truly prophets from God, they would have lived godly lives and encouraged the people to turn from their wickedness. Instead, they taught a popular "theology" that made it convenient for people to be religious and still live in sin.

Jehovah wasn't a local deity like the pagan idols, but a transcendent God who reigns above all things and fills heaven and earth (vv. 23-24). Nor was He blind like the idols (Ps. 115:5), unable to see the sins of the people. "Can any hide himself in secret places that I shall not see him?" (Jer. 23:24) Because they listened to the false prophets, the people believed lies about God, and what we believe about God determines how we live.

Finally, the false prophets were speaking *under a false inspiration (vv. 25-32).* They depended on dreams and delusions of the mind, and they even plagiarized messages from one another! Compared to the nourishing wheat of the Word, their messages were only straw; you couldn't eat it, build with it, or even be warmed by it.

The message of the true prophet is like a hammer that can tear down and build up (see 1:10) and even break the hardest rocks (23:29). The Word is like fire that consumes waste and purifies whatever it touches. Jeremiah had the Word burning in his heart (20:9; see Luke 24:32) and on his lips (Jer. 5:14). He was God's assayer, using the fire of the Word to test the lives of the people (6:27).

There are false prophets and teachers in our world today (2 Peter 2:1; 1 John 4:1-6), people who claim to know God's will because of their dreams, their study of astrology, or their special "spiritual" gifts. Some of them have invaded the church (Jude 3-4). Whatever anyone says who claims to be speaking for the Lord must be tested by the Word of God. "To the Law and to the testimony: if they speak not according to this word, it is because there is no light in them" (Isa. 8:20).

Their disrespectful attitude (vv. 33-40). The key Hebrew word in this section is *massa,* which means "a burden." Jeremiah used it to refer to bearing burdens on the Sabbath (Jer.

17:21-27), but in this context it means the burden of the message that the Lord places on His prophets (Nahum 1:1; Hab. 1:1; Mal. 1:1). For this reason, some scholars translate it "oracle," but "burden" is perfectly acceptable (see the NIV and NASB, both of which put "burden" in the margin).

God cautioned Jeremiah not to encourage the careless attitude of the priests, people, and false prophets when they asked him, "What is the burden of the Lord?" The phrase "burden of the Lord" was almost a cliché; it was used to poke fun at God's true prophet. (The phrase "born again" often gets the same kind of treatment.)

Why should the false prophets ask for an oracle from the Lord *when Jeremiah had already told them what God wanted them to hear?* If they hadn't obeyed what God already commanded, why should He tell them more? Their attitude toward God's message was careless and disrespectful; they weren't taking seriously God's message or God's messenger. The false prophets had distorted the truth to make it mean what they wanted it to mean, and yet they called their messages the "oracles of the Lord."

Jeremiah was to reply, "You are the burden!" (v. 33, NIV margin) *The Living Bible* catches the spirit of the passage:

> When one of the people or one of their "prophets" or priests asks you, "Well, Jeremiah, what is the sad news from the Lord today?" you shall reply, "What sad news? You are the sad news, for the Lord has cast you away!" (Jer. 23:33)

A worldly church puts an emphasis on "fun" and "entertainment" and forgets about tears. We now have "Christian comedians" who generate laughter for thirty minutes and then tack on the Gospel and give an invitation. While there's a proper place for humor in the Christian life, the church today needs to hear the words of James: "Lament and mourn and weep! Let your laughter be turned to mourning and your joy to gloom. Humble yourselves in the sight of the Lord, and He will lift you up" (James 4:9-10, NKJV). The church isn't taking God's Word seriously at an hour when the world is in serious trouble.

4. God disposes of His rebellious people (Jer. 24:1-10)

In 597 B.C., the Babylonians deported King Jehoiachin (also called Jeconiah or Coniah) along with many of the nobles and key citizens, leaving only the poorer people to work the land (2 Kings 24:14-16). It was the beginning of the end for Judah, and no doubt Jeremiah was greatly distressed.

Knowing that His servant needed encouragement, the Lord gave him a vision of two baskets of figs sitting before the temple of the Lord. One basket held very good figs, the kind that ripened early in the season, and the other basket contained rotten figs, which nobody could eat. Then the Lord explained that the good figs represented the exiles who had just been taken to Babylon, while the bad figs represented King Zedekiah and his officials as well as the survivors who remained in the land or who had fled to Egypt.

What do you do with rotten figs? You reject them and throw them away! What do you do with tasty good figs? You preserve them and enjoy them! God promised to care for the exiles, work in their hearts, and one day bring them back to their land. Jeremiah even wrote a letter to the exiles, telling them to live peaceably in the land and seek the Lord with all their hearts (Jer. 29:1-14). There was no future for King Zedekiah, who had succeeded Jehoiachin, or for the nobles that gave him such foolish counsel, but there was a future for a godly remnant that would seek the Lord with all their hearts.

In times of national catastrophe, no matter how discouraging the circumstances may be, God doesn't desert His faithful remnant. Rebels are scattered and destroyed, but true believers find God faithful to meet their needs and accomplish His great plans. The people who returned to the land after the Captivity were by no means perfect, but they had learned to trust the true and living God and not to worship idols. If the Captivity did nothing else, it purged the Jewish people of idolatry.

The destruction of Jerusalem and the fall of Judah were not accidents; they were appointments, for God was in control. Now the land would enjoy its Sabbaths (2 Chron. 36:21; Lev. 25:14ff), and the people exiled in Babylon would have time to repent and seek the Lord. In far off Babylon, God the Potter would remake His people (Jer. 18), and they would return to the land chastened and cleansed.

"No discipline seems pleasant at the time, but painful. Later on, however, it produces a harvest of righteousness and peace for those who have been trained by it" (Heb. 12:11, NIV).

EIGHT

JEREMIAH 25–29

Facing Truth and Fighting Lies

"An idealist believes the short run doesn't count. A cynic believes the long run doesn't matter. A realist believes that what is done or left undone in the short run determines the long run."

—Sidney J. Harris[1]

In these chapters, we see the prophet involved in four different ministry experiences as he served the Lord and sought to bring the kingdom of Judah back to God.

1. Jeremiah shares a secret (Jer. 25:1-38)

Jeremiah had been serving for twenty-three years when he delivered the messages recorded in chapters 25 and 26 (25:3; 26:1). He was called into prophetic service in the year 626 B.C. (1:2) and continued to minister after the fall of Jerusalem in 587 B.C., a period of over forty years. He was now at the midpoint of his career. When you consider the unsympathetic response of the people both to him and to his messages, you marvel that Jeremiah wasn't discouraged and ready to quit, but he continued to be faithful to his calling.

He delivered two messages—one to the Jews (vv. 1-14) and one to the Gentile nations (vv. 15-38).

Chastening for the people of Judah (vv. 1-14). Four times in this message, Jeremiah pronounced the solemn indictment, "You have not listened" (vv. 3-4, 7-8, NKJV). The earlier prophets, many of whom are unknown to us, had warned of great judgment if the nation didn't repent and turn to Jehovah, but their ministry went unheeded. Jeremiah had preached to the leaders and common people of Judah for twenty-three years and had received the same response. As they disobeyed the Law, worshiped idols, and rejected God's servants, the people deliberately provoked God to anger, and the day of His wrath was fast approaching.

Once again, Jeremiah announced that Nebuchadnezzar[2] and the armies of Babylon would be God's tool for punishing Judah (21:7, 10), and he dared to call the Babylonian king "My servant" (25:9; 27:6; 43:10). Nebuchadnezzar wasn't a believer in the true God of Israel, but in his conquests he was accomplishing God's will (51:20-23). God's own people wouldn't obey the Lord when they had everything to gain, but pagan rulers like Pharaoh (Rom. 9:17), Cyrus (Isa. 44:28; 45:1), and Nebuchadnezzar were servants of God to fulfill His purposes. The church today needs to remember that the Lord is sovereign and can use whatever tools He deigns to use to accomplish His purposes on earth, even unconverted leaders.

For the first time, Jeremiah shared the "secret" that the Captivity in Babylon would last seventy years (Jer. 25:11-14; 29:10; see Dan. 9:1-2). One reason God determined a period of seventy years was that the land might enjoy the rest that the Jews had denied it (2 Chron. 36:20-21; Lev. 25:3-5). The law of the Sabbatical Year had been ignored for nearly 500 years![3]

Judah, however, wouldn't be the only nation to suffer at the hands of the Babylonians, for "all these nations round about" (Jer. 25:9) would also be punished; among them the nations listed in 25:18-25 and 27:3. In one way or another, these nations were confederate with Judah against Babylon, but God's command was that the nations submit to Nebuchadnezzar. In fact, God would make *even the animals* obey the king of Babylon!

The end of the seventy years would mean not only freedom for the Jewish remnant but also judgment for the Babylonian Empire because of the ruthless way they treated both Jews and Gentiles (25:12-14). It was one thing for Nebuchadnezzar to do God's work, but when his attitude became proud and hateful, he overstepped his bounds. Babylon fell to the armies of the Medes and Persians in 539 B.C. (see Dan. 5).

Judgment for the Gentile nations (vv. 15-38). Jeremiah was called of God to minister not only to Judah but also to the other nations (Jer. 1:5). God had set him "over the nations" (v. 10) and given him authority to tell the Word of God. Though the Lord had not given His Law to the Gentile nations or entered into a covenant relationship with them, He still held them accountable for their sins (Rom. 1:18ff; Amos 1–2).

In this message, Jeremiah used eight vivid images to describe the judgment God was sending to the Gentiles.[4]

THE CUP OF WRATH (vv. 15-29). The psalmists used this familiar image of suffering and judgment (Pss. 60:3; 75:8), as well as the prophets (Isa. 29:9; 51:17, 22; 63:6; Jer. 25:15-16; 49:12; Ezek. 23:32-34; Hab. 2:16). You find the image repeated in the New Testament (Rev. 14:8-10; 16:19; 18:6). "Babylon was a golden cup in the Lord's hand that made all the earth drunk" (Jer. 51:7, NKJV).

Though this message centered mainly on the Gentiles, note that Jeremiah began his list with "Jerusalem, and the cities of Judah" (25:18); judgment begins with God's people (Ezek. 9:6; 1 Peter 4:17). "See, I am beginning to bring disaster on the city that bears My Name, and will you indeed go unpunished?" (Jer. 25:29, NIV)

How did Jeremiah make the various nations drink the cup of God's wrath? Certainly he didn't travel from nation to nation and meet with their leaders. There wasn't time for such an itinerary, and they wouldn't have welcomed him to their courts anyway. Perhaps he invited representatives of the various nations present in Jerusalem (see 27:3) to have a meal with him, preached his message to them, and then passed the cup around. It could have been another "action sermon" that would have gotten attention in the city, and when the foreign visitors returned to their own nations, they would have reported what the strange prophet in Jerusalem had said and done.

To drink a cup is a symbol of submission to the will of God. "The cup which My Father hath given Me, shall I not drink it?" (John 18:11) Jeremiah called the nations to submit to God's will, surrender to Nebuchadnezzar, and be spared destruction. Jeremiah would later illustrate this message by wearing a yoke (Jer. 27). If the nations didn't drink the cup of submission, they would end up drinking the cup of judgment and "get drunk and vomit, and fall, to rise no more" (25:27, NIV).

THE ROARING LION (vv. 30a, 38). Lions roar to paralyze their prey with fear, and God will roar in judgment when He visits the nations (see Hosea 11:10; Joel 3:16; Amos 1:2; 3:8). God had spoken in love to His people, but they refused to obey. Now He must speak in wrath. In the last days, the Lamb of God will become like the lion and pour out His wrath on a wicked world (Rev. 5:5-7).

THE WINEPRESS (v. 30B). This is another familiar metaphor for judgment (Isa. 63:3; Joel 3:13; Rev. 14:19-20). As they shared in the joy of the harvest, those treading the grapes shouted and sang to one another (Isa. 16:10), but God would do the shouting as He judged the nations that had resisted His will.

THE LAWSUIT (v. 31). "The Lord will bring charges against the nations" (NIV; see Hosea 4:1; Micah 6:2). The Lord first brought charges against His own people for abandoning Him and turning to idols (Jer. 2:9-13). In this "trial" there would be a Judge but no jury, an indictment but no defense, and a sentence but no appeal. God had given His people plenty of opportunity to admit their guilt and repent, but they refused. Now it was too late.

THE STORM (vv. 32-33). Like a tornado, Nebuchadnezzar's army would move from nation to nation and city to city and leave only devastation behind. "Behold a whirlwind of the Lord has gone forth in fury—a violent whirlwind! It will fall violently on the head of the wicked" (23:19, NKJV; see 30:23; Isa. 30:30).

THE REFUSE (v. 33). Not to have a proper burial was a disgrace, for then the body was being treated like common rubbish (8:2; 9:22; 16:4; 22:19). The Hebrew word means "dung," which is even worse (see Isa. 25:10-11, NIV).

THE BROKEN POTTERY (v. 34). "You will fall and be shattered like fine pottery" (NIV). This reminds us of Jeremiah's "action sermon" when he publicly broke the clay vessel (Jer. 19:1-13; see also 13:14; 48:38). One day, Jesus Christ shall break the nations like so many clay pots (Ps. 2:9). The Hebrew word translated "pleasant vessel" (Jer. 25:34) refers to fine pottery and not just common pots. God wants His vessels to be clean and yielded. If they aren't, He has the right to smash them.

THE SLAUGHTERED FLOCK (vv. 34-38). The shepherds were the leaders of the nation—kings and nobles, priests and false prophets—who had exploited God's flock and not compassionately cared for God's people. Now it was time for *them* to be slaughtered, and there would be no place for them to hide!

Instead of hearing the cries of the sheep, the shepherds would hear their own wailing as they saw their pasture (Judah) destroyed. Like a fierce lion (v. 38; see v. 30), God would leap out on the shepherds and the sheep, and there would be no escape.

"For the time is come that judgment must begin at the house of God: and if it first begin at us, what shall the end be of them that obey not the Gospel of God?" (1 Peter 4:17)

2. Jeremiah risks his life (Jer. 26:1-24)

This chapter should be studied in connection with chapter 7, because they both deal with Jeremiah's courageous sermon given in the temple. The sermon is summarized in verses 3-7, and you will note the emphasis on *hearing the Word of God* (see 25:3-8). Jeremiah preached exactly what God commanded him to preach and didn't alter the message in order to please the people. The false prophets preached what the people *wanted* to hear, but Jeremiah preached what the people *needed* to hear. "Whatever I command thee thou shalt speak" (1:7).

The people in the temple, however, encouraged by the priests and false prophets, rejected Jeremiah's message and treated him like a false prophet who deserved to die. To them, it was blasphemous for Jeremiah to declare that Jehovah would allow the holy city and His holy temple to fall into the defiling and destructive hands of the heathen the way the ark at Shiloh fell into the hands of the Philistines (1 Sam. 4). Since God's covenant with David protected the city and the temple, Jeremiah was actually denying the covenant! He was leading the people astray and deserved to die (Deut. 18:20).

Receiving a report about a tumult in the temple, the officials left the palace and came to the temple to see what was occurring. (This reminds us of Paul's experience recorded in Acts 21:27-40.) After hearing the people, priests, and prophets charge Jeremiah with blasphemy, they gave the prophet opportunity to speak. Jeremiah then presented three arguments in his defense.

First, what he had spoken was commanded by the Lord because the Lord had sent him (Jer. 26:12, 15). If they killed him, they were killing one of God's prophets, and he would rather be faithful to God and die than unfaithful and live. Second, *they* were the ones in danger; he was the one seeking to rescue them! (v. 13) If they repented and obeyed God's Word, the Lord would relent of His plans to judge the nation and would deliver them. Third, if they killed him, they would shed innocent blood, and that would only make their impending judgment worse.

Three factors led to Jeremiah's release. First, having heard the evidence, the officials decided that the accusations were false and that Jeremiah should not die (v. 16). Second, some of the wise elders of the city argued the case further by citing a precedent: the ministry of the Prophet Micah in the days of King Hezekiah (vv. 18-19; Micah 1:1; 3:12). At that time, the Assyrians were threatening Jerusalem (Isa. 36–37), but Hezekiah obeyed the Lord and led the people in confession and repentance. Third, Ahikam, one of the officials, proved a friend to Jeremiah and effected his release (Jer. 26:24). Ahikam had served King Josiah (2 Kings 22:11-14) and was the father of Gedaliah, the future governor of Judah (25:22; 40:5ff).[5]

On first reading, the illustration of Uriah (Jer. 26:20-23) seems out of place as a defense of Jeremiah, for the king had executed Uriah the prophet after he had fled to Egypt, and been brought back to King Jehoiakim. On the other hand, Jeremiah stayed in the land of Judah and even ministered in the precincts of the temple! Jeremiah gave every evidence of being a loyal citizen, even though he disagreed with the politics of the leaders of the government. Although we can't fault him for trying to save his own life, Uriah had broken the law while trying to prophesy God's truth, and this led to his own death.

3. Jeremiah wears a yoke (Jer. 27:1–28:17)[6]

Once again, Jeremiah had to use an "action sermon" to get the attention of the people, and he did it at a time when Zedekiah was conferring with representatives from five neighboring nations. These nations were allies of Judah, and together they were planning a strategy for dealing with Nebuchadnezzar.

The message of the yoke (vv. 1-22). A yoke speaks of submission, and that's the message Jeremiah was trying to get across. First, Jeremiah sent the message to *the envoys of the nations (vv. 1-11).* What these politicians needed was not clever strategy but submission to Babylon. When Jeremiah was asked why he was wearing a yoke,[7] he gave them the message from God: Judah and the other nations must submit to Nebuchadnezzar or else be destroyed. God had given the nations to the king of Babylon, and those nations who rebelled against him were rebelling against God (vv. 7-8, 11-12). He sent this message to the envoys gathered in Jerusalem, who certainly had heard about this peculiar Jewish man who was walking around wearing a yoke (see 28:10).

"And all nations shall serve him [Nebuchadnezzar], and his son, and his son's son" is a proverbial expression that simply means "they shall serve him for a long time." Nebuchadnezzar's son Evil-Merodach did succeed him (52:31-34; 2 Kings 25:27), but he was followed by his brother-in-law Nergal-Sharezer (Jer. 39:3, 39), not by Nebuchadnezzar's grandson.

Judah had its false prophets, and the Gentile nations had their diviners (people who read omens), dreamers (those who interpret dreams), and enchanters and sorcerers (those who collaborate with demons in order to discover or control the future), but neither Judah nor the Gentile nations dared to listen to these purveyors of lies. Since dabbling in the occult was forbidden to the Jews (Lev. 19:26; Deut. 18:10-11), why would Zedekiah want to listen to political counsel from the pit of hell? (See 2 Cor. 6:14-18.)

Jeremiah then gave the same message *to King Zedekiah (Jer. 27:12-15).* Since the king had rebelled against Babylon and refused to pay tribute, he was now in serious trouble. When the king saw Jeremiah wearing the yoke, he surely must have gotten the message: "Bring your necks under the yoke of the king of Babylon, and serve him and his people, and live" (v. 12). Jeremiah warned the king not to listen to the deceptive messages of the false prophets, because they were speaking only lies in the name of the Lord.

Jeremiah then delivered the "yoke message" to *the priests and the people (vv. 16-22).* The false prophets were claiming that the valuable articles of gold and bronze that the Babylonians had taken from the temple would soon be returned to Jerusalem, but Jeremiah knew this was a lie.[8] Actually, these treasures weren't brought back until God visited the Jews and the remnant returned to Judah after the decree of Cyrus (Ezra 1–2). The important thing wasn't to rescue the temple furnishings but to save the people from death and the city from destruction. This could be done only if the nation submitted to the king of Babylon.

Jeremiah taunted the false prophets by encouraging them to pray about the matter. After all, if they were true prophets of God, the Lord would surely answer their prayers. He told them to pray, not for the return of the treasures now in Babylon, but for the preservation of the treasures still in the temple. When the Babylonians organized a second deportation in 597 at the beginning of Zedekiah's reign (Jer. 27:1; 28:1), it proved that the false prophets were indeed liars and that their prayers weren't answered.

Jeremiah ended his message to the priests and people with a promise of hope: At the end of the seventy years of captivity, God would visit His people in Babylon and bring them back to their land. Even in wrath, God remembers mercy (Hab. 3:2).

The breaking of the yoke (vv. 1-17). While Jeremiah was wearing the yoke and calling the nation to submit to Babylon, Hananiah, one of the false prophets, confronted him in the temple. About this same time, according to historians, Nebuchadnezzar was putting down a revolt in his own land. Hananiah wrongly interpreted the uprising as the end of Nebuchadnezzar's rule. Hananiah announced that God had broken the yoke of the king of Babylon and that the temple treasures would be returned to Jerusalem within two years. More than that, King Jeconiah and all the exiles would be returned with them.

These messages contradicted what Jeremiah had spoken in the name of the Lord. The Lord had told Jeremiah that the deported people and the temple vessels wouldn't be restored to the land until He visited the exiles at the end of their seventy-year captivity (Jer. 27:16-22). Furthermore, King Jeconiah would never return to Judah but would die in Babylon (22:24-27; 52:31-34).

Jeremiah's response to Hananiah's message was "Amen, so be it! May the Lord fulfill what you have promised!" How are we to interpret this reply? Certainly not as agreement with what the false prophet had said, because Jeremiah knew better. Perhaps we might paraphrase Jeremiah's words, "Oh, that the Lord would do what you have said! This would make me very happy!" But Jeremiah knew that Hananiah's prophecy of peace wouldn't be fulfilled. If it were fulfilled, this would contradict all that the prophets had predicted who had preceded them, for they prophesied judgment.

Hananiah became angry, removed Jeremiah's yoke, and broke it before the people. If Jeremiah could preach "action sermons," so could Hananiah! "Thus saith the Lord," he announced. "Even so will I break the yoke of Nebuchadnezzar king of Babylon from the neck of all nations within the space of two full years" (28:11). Not only would Judah be set free, but also *all nations* would remove the yoke of Babylon. Again, this contradicted the message Jeremiah had preached to the nations.

Jeremiah didn't resist Hananiah when he removed the yoke, nor did he reply to the false prophet's message. "And the Prophet Jeremiah went his way" (v. 11). The priests and people witnessing this dramatic scene may have interpreted Jeremiah's silence as agreement, but Jeremiah was only waiting for the right message from the Lord and the right time to deliver it.

The message to Hananiah was both national and personal. As far as the nation was concerned, because they would follow his deceptive counsel, an iron yoke would replace the wooden yoke (see Deut. 28:48). The nations would not escape; Nebuchadnezzar would enslave them. It's always the case that when we reject the light yoke of God's will, we end up wearing a heavier yoke of our own making. The personal message was that the false prophet would die before the year was up, and two months later, he did (Jer. 28:1, 17). But even this striking event didn't awaken the hearts of the people, for they were bent on doing evil.

God doesn't usually strike people dead in such a dramatic fashion, but it did happen to the followers of Korah (Num. 16), to Uzzah (2 Sam. 6), to the Assyrian army (2 Kings 19:35), and to Ananias and Sapphira (Acts 5). "It is a fearful thing to fall into the hands of the living God" (Heb. 10:31).

4. Jeremiah writes some letters (Jer. 29:1-32)

Several different letters are involved in this chapter: a letter from Jeremiah to the exiles (vv. 1-14); a letter concerning

Jewish false prophets in Babylon to which Jeremiah replied (vv. 15-23); a letter from Shemaiah to the temple priests concerning Jeremiah, which he read (vv. 24-29); and a letter from Jeremiah to the exiles concerning Shemaiah (vv. 30-32). Correspondence like this wasn't difficult to maintain in those days, for there were regular diplomatic missions between Jerusalem and Babylon (v. 3), and Jeremiah had friends in high places in the government.

Jeremiah's word of encouragement (vv. 1-14).[9] Sometime after the deportation in 597, Jeremiah sent a letter to the exiles in Babylon to tell them how to behave in their new land. A man with the heart of a true shepherd, Jeremiah wanted to enlighten them and encourage them in their life in Babylon. Governed by special laws concerning "clean" and "unclean" things, the Jewish people would have a difficult time adjusting to a pagan society. Jeremiah wanted them to be good witnesses to the idolatrous Babylonians, and he also wanted them to be good Jews even though separated from their temple and its services. He addressed himself to the needs of three kinds of people.

THOSE WITH NO HOPE (vv. 4-6). The exiles had lost everything but their lives and what few possessions they could carry with them to Babylon. They'd lost their freedom and were now captives. They'd been taken from their homes and had lost their means of making a living. They were separated from relatives and friends, some of whom may have perished in the long march from Jerusalem to Babylon. No matter how they looked at it, the situation seemed hopeless.

How should we handle such a depressing situation? *Accept it from the hand of God (v. 4) and let God have His way.* It does no good to hang our harps on the willow trees and sit around and weep, although this may be a temporary normal reaction to tragedy (Ps. 137:1-4). One of the first steps in turning tragedy into triumph is to accept the situation courageously and put ourselves into the hands of a loving God, who makes no mistakes.

THOSE WITH FALSE HOPES (Jer. 29:6-9). The false prophets had convinced the people that the stay in Babylon would be a brief one, perhaps two years (vv. 8-9). Thus, there was no need to settle down and try to resume a normal life, but Jeremiah told them just the opposite. Since they would be there as long as seventy years (v. 10), there was plenty of time to build houses and set up homes. It was important that the exiles have families so there would be people available to return to Judea when the Captivity ended. This small Jewish remnant was holding in its hands the future of God's great plan of salvation, and they must obey Him, be fruitful, and multiply (v. 6).

It would be easy for the Jews to wage constant warfare against their idolatrous Gentile captors, but Jeremiah instructed them to strive to get along with the Babylonians. The exiles were to be peacemakers, not troublemakers, and they were to pray sincerely for their enemies (Matt. 5:43-48; 1 Tim. 2:1-3; Titus 3:1-2). It was possible to be good Jews even in a pagan land. Remember, if we reject the wooden yoke of submission, we end up wearing only an iron yoke of subjugation (Jer. 28:12-14). Thus, the best course is to yield ourselves to the Lord and to those who are over us, no matter how badly they may treat us. (See Peter's counsel to Christian slaves in 1 Peter 2:18-25.) To indulge in false hopes is to miss what God has planned for us.

THOSE WHO HAVE TRUE HOPE (vv. 10-14). True hope is based on the revealed Word of God, not on the "dream messages" of self-appointed prophets (v. 10, NIV). God gave His people a "gracious promise" (v. 10, NIV) to deliver them, and He would keep His promise. God makes His plans for His people, and they are good plans that ultimately bring hope and peace. Therefore, there is no need to be afraid or discouraged.

In every situation, however, God's people have the responsibility to seek the Lord, pray, and ask Him to fulfill His promises, for the Word and prayer go together (Acts 6:4). The purpose of chastening is that we might seek the Lord, confess our sins, and draw near to Him (Heb. 12:3-13). According to Jeremiah 29:14, these promises reach beyond the Jews captive in Babylon and include all of Israel throughout the world. Jeremiah was looking ahead to the end of the age when Israel will be regathered to meet their Messiah and enter their kingdom (Isa. 10:20–12:6).

Jeremiah's word of explanation (vv. 15-23). The false prophets in Babylon were giving false hopes to the people concerning Jerusalem and Judah, and this word got back to Jeremiah. Yes, King Zedekiah was still on the throne and there were Jews still living in Jerusalem, but this was no guarantee that the city and the nation would be delivered. The people still in the land were the "bad figs" that would be thrown out (Jer. 29:17; see chap. 24). The important thing wasn't what happened to the people in the land but what the exiles would do with the Word of God. If they obeyed God, He would work out His purposes and bless them.

Jeremiah named two of the false prophets, Ahab and Zedekiah, who not only preached lies to the people but also lived godless lives. Consequently, he announced their doom in Babylon. Their names would become proverbs in Israel, warning not to rebel against the Word of God.

Jeremiah's word of warning (vv. 24-32). This warning was in response to Shemaiah, another false prophet in Babylon, who had written letters to people in Jerusalem "in the name of the Lord," urging them to imprison Jeremiah because he was a madman. The chief temple officer Zephaniah let Jeremiah read the letter (see 21:1). Because Shemaiah had a following in Babylon, Jeremiah warned the exiles that the man was a rebel against God and that the Lord had neither sent him nor given him a message. Shemaiah would be judged for his sins by dying childless in Babylon, never to see his native land again.

What life does to us depends largely on what life finds in us. If we seek the Lord and want His best, then circumstances will build us and prepare us for what He has planned. If we rebel or if we look for quick and easy shortcuts, then circumstances will destroy us and rob us of the future God wants us to enjoy. The same sun that melts the ice also hardens the clay.

God's thoughts and plans concerning us come from His heart and lead to His peace. Why look for substitutes?

NINE

JEREMIAH 30–33

The God Who Makes Things New

"A small man can see when it is growing dark . . . but he cannot see beyond the darkness. He does not know how to put a sunbeam into his picture. A great man pierces the darkness and sees the glory of a hidden dawn."

—Charles E. Jefferson[1]

Bible scholars often call these four chapters "The Book of Consolation." In them, the Lord amplified the wonderful promise He gave to His people in the letter Jeremiah sent the Babylonian exiles:

> "For I know the plans I have for you," declares the Lord, "plans to prosper you and not to harm you, plans to give you hope and a future" (29:11, NIV).

Jeremiah 30–33 describes the glory of the dawning of a new day for the people of Israel, not only for the exiles in Babylon but also for the Jewish people in the latter days before the

Lord returns. As you study, you'll discover that Jeremiah had two "horizons" in view: the nearer horizon of the return of the exiles to Judah and the farther horizon of the regathering of Israel in the end times from the nations of the earth.

1. Redemption: a new beginning (Jer. 30:1-24)

Jeremiah received the words recorded in 30:1–31:25 while he was asleep (31:26), for God sometimes spoke to His servants through dreams (Dan. 10:9; Zech. 4:1). God instructed Jeremiah to write His words in a book (scroll) so the nation would have a permanent record of the promises God was giving to His people (see Jer. 36:1-4).

In His instructions to Jeremiah, God stated the theme of His message: Israel (the Northern Kingdom, taken by Assyria in 722 B.C.) and Judah (the Southern Kingdom) will eventually return to their land as a united people (30:3). While this promise refers ultimately to the regathering of the Jews at the end of the age, it certainly was an encouragement to the exiles in Babylon, for if God can gather His people from *all* the nations of the world, surely He can deliver Judah from the captivity of *one* nation. (Note His promise in v. 10.)

This "redemption" of His people from bondage is pictured in several ways.

The broken yoke (vv. 4-11). "For it shall come to pass in that day . . . that I will break his yoke from your neck, and will burst your bonds; foreigners shall no more enslave them" (v. 8, NKJV). When the prophets used the phrase "in that day," they were usually referring to the future time when God will judge the nations of the world and restore the Jews to their land.[2]

Before Israel is delivered, however, all the nations of the earth will experience "the time of Jacob's trouble" (v. 7), a phrase that describes the time of tribulation that will come upon the earth (Matt. 24:21-31; Mark 13:19-27; Rev. 6–19). A frequent biblical symbol of suffering is a woman in travail (Jer. 30:6), and this image is used to describe the Tribulation in the end times (see Isa. 13:8 and context; Micah 4:9-13; 1 Thes. 5:1-3).[3]

The promise in Jeremiah 30:9 applies to the future Kingdom Age, following the Tribulation, when the Messiah shall reign over His people. You find corresponding promises in 23:5 and 33:14-26. When Jesus was here on earth, His people said, "We will not have this man to reign over us" (Luke 19:14), but in that day, they will recognize their Messiah-King and welcome Him (Zech. 12:8–14:21).

The healed wound (vv. 12-17). In Isaiah's day, Judah was a "sick" nation (Isa. 1:5-6), and thanks to the superficial ministry of the false prophets (Jer. 6:14; 8:11), the sickness became worse in Jeremiah's day (10:19; 14:17; 15:18). The wounds on the "body politic" were so bad that there was no medicine that could cure the nation, and the allies ("lovers") that the Jewish leaders trusted abandoned Judah to her fate. The Lord reminded the Jews that it was He who used other nations to wound them because of their disobedience to Him (30:14). He used Assyria to chasten Israel and Babylon to punish Judah, and in the latter days, He will use the Gentile nations to correct Israel and prepare the Jews for the return of their Messiah. However, God will punish the Gentile nations for the way they treat Israel in the last days (v. 16; see Joel 3) just as He punished Assyria and Babylon. "But I will restore you to health and heal your wounds" was God's encouraging promise (Jer. 30:17, NIV).

The calm after the storm (vv. 18-24). Jeremiah then picked up the image of the storm (v. 23) that he had used earlier (23:19-20) to describe the Babylonian assault, but now he related it to the trials of "the latter days" (30:24). God promised that Jerusalem and the cities of Judah will be rebuilt[4] and that the fortunes of the people will be restored. Their mourning will turn to joy and their children will again enjoy a normal life.

Instead of being under despotic Gentile rulers, the Jews will have the Messiah as their ruler—"one of their own" (v. 21, NIV), that is, a Jew. But here's a surprising revelation: Not only will the Messiah be their King, but He will also be their Priest! "Then I will cause Him to draw near, and He shall approach Me" (v. 21, NKJV). This is language that applies especially to the Jewish high priest, who alone entered the holy of holies on the annual Day of Atonement (Lev. 16). Only Jesus Christ, who is both King and Priest (Heb. 7–8), can qualify to fulfill this prophecy.

To summarize: The people of Judah and Jerusalem will experience terrible trials at the hands of the Babylonians. They will end up wearing the Gentile yoke, bearing the wounds caused by their sins, and having endured the storm of God's wrath. But God would eventually deliver them, breaking the yoke, healing the wounds, and bringing peace after the storm. All of this will be a foreshadowing of what will happen to the Jews in the end times as they go through the Tribulation, meet their Messiah-King, and enter into their kingdom.

2. Reconciliation: a new people (Jer. 31:1-30)

A nation is more than its land and cities; it's people living together, working together, and worshiping together. In this chapter, Jeremiah described the people of God and the new things the Lord would do for them. He first spoke to a united nation (vv. 1, 27-30), then to Israel (vv. 2-20), and finally to Judah (vv. 21-26).

A united people (vv. 1, 27-30). Because of the sins of Solomon and the foolishness of his son Rehoboam, the Jewish nation divided and became Israel and Judah, the Northern Kingdom and the Southern Kingdom (2 Kings 11–12). But in the last days, the Lord will gather His people, unite them, and be "the God of all the families of Israel" (Jer. 31:1). In fact, God compared Israel and Judah to seed that will be sown in the land and produce one harvest, not two (v. 27).

Jeremiah's ministry included breaking down and plucking up as well as building and planting (1:10); up to this point, it had been primarily the former. In the future, however, God will build and plant so the people and the land could be restored. There would be no more "blaming the fathers" for what happened (Ezek. 18:1-4, 19-23; Deut. 24:16), for each person will take responsibility for his or her own sins. This principle certainly had application to the remnant that returned to the land after the Captivity, for it was the failure of *individuals* to obey God that caused the ruin of the nation. If the kings and priests had been like Josiah and Jeremiah, the nation could have been saved.

A restored Israel (vv. 2-20). The names "Ephraim" and "Samaria" are references to the Northern Kingdom of Israel, whose capital was at Samaria (Jer. 31:4-6, 9, 18, 20). The people of the Northern Kingdom were captured in 722 B.C. by the Assyrians, who brought other peoples into the land so as to produce a mixed race (2 Kings 17). When the people of Judah returned to their land from the Captivity, they would have nothing to do with the Samaritans (Ezra 4:1-4; Neh. 2:19-20; 13:28), a practice that persisted into New Testament times (John 4:9).[5] Subsequently, the Samaritans established their own religion, temple, and priesthood, and this alienated the Jews even more.

The promises recorded in Jeremiah 31:2-22 don't apply to Ephraim/Israel after the Captivity, because the Samaritans weren't a part of the rebuilding of the land. These promises apply to the scattered Ten Tribes[6] in the end times when God will call the Jews together and restore them to their land. Then there will be one nation, and the Samaritans will worship, not on Mt. Gerizim, but on Mt. Zion (v. 6; John 4:20-24). Jeremiah pictured God summoning His family and gathering His flock, leading them out of the desert into the fruitful garden. Since none of this happened after the Captivity, we can assume it will occur in the end times when Ephraim repents and turns to the Lord (Jer. 31:18-20). As you read these promises, notice the emphasis on singing, praise, and joy.

Matthew later referred to verses 15-17 (Matt. 2:16-18). Rachel was the mother of Joseph and Benjamin, and Joseph was the father of Ephraim and Manasseh, the two leading tribes in the Northern Kingdom (Gen. 30:22-24). Jeremiah heard Rachel weeping at Ramah, where the Jewish prisoners were assembled for their long journey to Babylon (Jer. 40:1). Her descendants through Joseph had been captured by the Assyrians, and now her descendants through Benjamin (the Southern Kingdom) were going to Babylon. Her labor as a mother had been in vain! (Remember, Rachel died giving birth to Benjamin.) But God assured her that both Ephraim and Judah will be restored (31:16-17), and therefore her sacrifices will not have been in vain.[7]

A restored Judah (vv. 21-26). As the Jews started for Babylon, God instructed them to remember the roads and set up markers along the route, for the people would use those same roads when they return to their land. Jeremiah pictured Judah as a silly girl, flitting from lover to lover, and now summoned to come home. (He used this image before. See 2:1-2, 20; 3:1-11.) According to the Law, a daughter who prostituted herself should have been killed (Lev. 21:9; Deut. 22:21), but God would do a new thing: He would welcome her home and forgive her!

The phrase "a woman shall compass a man" (Jer. 31:22; "surround" in NIV) has been given so many interpretations that to examine them all is to invite confusion. The word translated "compass" also means "to surround with care, to shield"; it's used of God's care for Israel in the wilderness (Deut. 32:10). The word for "man" means "a strong man, a champion," so the "new thing" God does is make the women so strong that they protect the men! (Keep in mind that this was a strongly masculine society.) In other words, the return of the exiles won't be a parade of weak stragglers; it will be the march of warriors, including the women, who were considered too weak to fight in that day.[8]

This is a picture of that future regathering of the people of Israel in the end times. They will enjoy a renewed land, where the citizens will bless their neighbors in the name of the Lord. Farmers and city dwellers will live together in harmony because of the blessing of the Lord.

3. Regeneration: a new covenant (Jer. 31:31-40)

Any plan for the betterment of human society that ignores the sin problem is destined to failure. It isn't enough to change the environment, for the heart of every problem is the problem of the heart. God must change the hearts of people so that they want to love Him and do His will. That's why He announced a New Covenant to replace the Old Covenant under which the Jews had lived since the days of Moses, a covenant that could direct their conduct but not change their character.

Jewish history is punctuated with a number of "covenant renewals" that brought temporary blessing but didn't change the hearts of the people. The Book of Deuteronomy records a renewal of the covenant under Moses, before the people entered the Promised Land. In addition, before he died, Joshua led the people in reaffirming the covenant (Josh. 23–24). Samuel called the nation to renew their vows to God (1 Sam. 12), and both Hezekiah (2 Chron. 29–31) and Josiah (2 Chron. 34–35) inspired great days of "revival" as they led the people back to God's Law.

The fact that the blessings didn't last is no argument against times of revival and refreshing. When somebody told Billy Sunday that revivals weren't necessary because they didn't last, the evangelist replied, "A bath doesn't last, but it's good to have one occasionally." A nation that is built on spiritual and moral principles must have frequent times of renewal or the foundations will crumble.

But the New Covenant isn't just another renewal of the Old Covenant that God gave at Sinai; it's a covenant that's new in every way. The New Covenant is *inward* so that God's Law is written on the heart and not on stone tablets (2 Cor. 3; Ezek. 11:19-20; 18:31; 36:26-27). The emphasis is *personal* rather than national, with each person putting faith in the Lord and receiving a "new heart" and with it a new disposition toward godliness.

The Old Covenant tried to control conduct, but the New Covenant changes character so that people can love the Lord and one another and want to obey God's will. "By the Law is the knowledge of sin" (Rom. 3:20), but under the New Covenant God promised "I will forgive their iniquity, and I will remember their sin no more" (Jer. 31:34). It is this covenant that the Jews will experience in the last days when they see their Messiah and repent (Zech. 12:10–13:1).

The basis for the New Covenant is the work of Jesus Christ on the cross (Matt. 26:27-28; Mark 14:22-24; Luke 22:19-20). Because the church today partakes in Israel's spiritual riches (Rom. 11:12-32; Eph. 3:1-6), anyone who puts faith in Jesus Christ shares in this New Covenant (Heb. 8:6-13; 10:14-18). It's an experience of regeneration, being "born again" into the family of God (John 3:1-21).

The Lord also affirmed the permanence of the nation and the faithfulness of His relationship to His people (Jer. 31:35-37). It would be easier for the sun to stop shining and the moon and stars to go out than for God to break His promises to His people Israel. Just as Jerusalem was rebuilt after the Babylonian Captivity, so it will be restored after the "time of Jacob's trouble" and be holy to the Lord. Because of its ancient associations with Israel, Islam, Jesus, and the church, Jerusalem is called "the holy city," but it will not truly be holy until the Lord restores it and reigns in glory at the end of the age.

4. Restoration: a new land and kingdom (Jer. 32:1–33:26)

It wasn't enough for the prophet merely to preach God's promises; he also had to practice them and prove to his hearers that he believed them himself. "Faith without works is dead" (James 2:26). Therefore, God directed Jeremiah to give another "action sermon" and purchase a piece of property at a time when the fortunes of Judah couldn't have been lower. In so doing, Jeremiah got the attention of the people and was able to affirm God's great promises to them. He had to "put his money where his mouth was" and God blessed him for it.

An "illogical thing" (vv. 1-44). The tenth year of Zedekiah's rule was 587 B.C., one year before Jerusalem fell to the Babylonians, when Jeremiah was confined in the court of the prison (37:21). King Zedekiah didn't like Jeremiah's messages concerning himself and the city (32:3-5), but perhaps his imprisoning the prophet was God's way of protecting Jeremiah from his enemies and providing food for him during the terrible siege. People can imprison God's workers, but God's Word is not bound (2 Tim. 2:9). God's Word came to Jeremiah telling him to do a most illogical thing: Buy a piece of the battlefield!

THE TRANSACTION (vv. 6-15). God told Jeremiah that his cousin Hanamel was coming with an offer to sell property in their hometown of Anathoth. If Hanamel had suddenly shown up, Jeremiah probably would have refused the offer. After all, the field was in the hands of the Babylonians, Jeremiah was in prison, and the future of the nation was bleak indeed. Of what use would a field be to Jeremiah who couldn't possibly live for another seventy years?

That, however, is what faith is all about: obeying God in spite of what we see, how we feel, and what may happen. It's well been said that faith is not believing in spite of evidence but obeying in spite of consequence, and Jeremiah's actions illustrate that maxim. When word got out that Jeremiah was investing in worthless real estate, many people must have laughed, others shook their heads in disbelief, and some probably thought he was crazy.

The transaction was probably carried out in the court of the prison with all things done legally. Jeremiah signed the deeds, paid the money, and gave the legal documents to his secretary Baruch, who is mentioned here for the first time.[9] The witnesses attested to the signature and the deeds and probably went away wondering whether Jeremiah had lost his mind. The transaction was the talk of the city, you can be sure, with Hanamel the hero. Hanamel may have thought he engineered a shrewd deal, but he only gave evidence of his unbelief.

THE REACTION (vv. 16-25). As was often the case with Jeremiah, a testing experience of doubt followed a triumphant experience of faith. Having obeyed God's command by faith, Jeremiah was now wondering how God would ever give him his property; he did the right thing by praying about it. The best way to handle doubt is to talk to God, be honest about your feelings, and then wait for Him to give you His message from His Word.

True prayer begins with worship (vv. 17-19) and focuses on the greatness of God. No matter what our problems are, God is greater; and the more we see His greatness, the less threatening our problems will become. True prayer also involves rehearsing what God has done for us in the past and remembering how He kept His promises and met the needs of His people (vv. 20-23). Jeremiah's prayer concluded with the prophet sharing his difficult situation with God and turning it over to Him (vv. 24-25). Outside the city was the besieging Babylonian army; within the city were famine, disease, and disobedience; and in Jeremiah's heart was a nagging doubt that he'd made a fool of himself.

THE CONFIRMATION (vv. 26-44). God met the needs of His servant and confirmed that his decisions were right. The basic theme of Jeremiah's prayer was "Nothing is too hard for You" (v. 17, NIV), and God reaffirmed that very truth to His servant (v. 27).[10] Good theology always leads to a confident heart if we put our trust in the Word, for "faith comes by hearing, and hearing by the Word of God" (Rom. 10:17, NKJV).

The Lord's reply to Jeremiah affirmed what He had told him in the past: The city was heading for certain destruction because of the repeated sins of the people (Jer. 32:28-35). Their sin of idolatry had provoked the Lord, and the only solution was to put them in the land of Babylon and give them their fill of idols. Because the people had resisted the prophets and refused to obey the Law, they would have to take the consequences.

The Lord then affirmed to Jeremiah that the situation wasn't lost, for He would gather His people and bring them back to their land (vv. 36-44). This promise seems to apply to the end times when Israel will be gathered "out of all countries" (v. 37) and the New Covenant will be in force, for the people will have a changed heart toward the Lord. Next, Jeremiah heard the word that gave him joy: "And fields shall be bought in this land" (v. 43). The day would come when Jeremiah's purchase would be validated and his "action sermon" vindicated!

The application of this Scripture for today's believer is obvious: The world laughs at us for our faith and our investments in the future, but one day God will keep His promises and vindicate us before people and angels. Instead of living for the sinful pleasures of this present world, we seek the joys of the world to come. We refuse to sacrifice the eternal for the temporal. The unbelieving world may ridicule us, but ultimately God will vindicate His people.

"Unsearchable things" (33:1-26). "Call to Me and I will answer you and tell you great and unsearchable things you do not know" (v. 3, NIV). The word translated "unsearchable" pictures an impregnable city protected by high walls—an apt image during the siege of Jerusalem. The idea is that God's people don't learn the hidden things of the Lord by "storming the gates" through their own strength but by seeking Him through believing prayer. Because Jeremiah asked the Lord to teach him, God showed him "hidden things" that related to the future of his people. The prophet knew that the city was destined for judgment (vv. 4-5), but the Lord gave him further words of assurance and encouragement—promises that relate to the end times.

The defiled nation would be healed and cleansed (vv. 6-8), and the disgraceful city would bring joy and renown to the Lord and be a testimony to all the nations of the world of the marvelous goodness and grace of God (v. 9). The deserted city would one day be filled with people praising the Lord and expressing their joy to one another (vv. 10-11). The pasture lands, ruined by devastating judgment, would one day be full of flocks and herds, and the little towns would once more enjoy happiness (vv. 12-13). Since these blessings didn't come during the post-exilic period, we have to believe they'll be realized when the Lord returns and restores His people and their land.

The greatest blessing of all will be their promised King reigning in righteousness! (vv. 14-16; see 23:5) Jeremiah already told us that His name is "The Lord our Righteousness" (v. 6), but now God revealed that *Jerusalem will bear the same name!* That certainly didn't happen when the exiles returned to rebuild their temple and their city. Therefore, this promise is for the latter days. Then when people call Jerusalem "the holy city," the name will be appropriate.

Once again, the Lord used the faithfulness of His "creation covenant" (Gen. 8:22) to undergird the dependability of His promises and the perpetuity of His people (Jer. 33:19-26; see 31:35-37). But He adds something else: He will multiply the people as the stars of the heaven, which was one of the promises He had made to Abraham (Gen. 15:1-5).[11]

"For I will restore their fortunes and have compassion on them" (Jer. 33:26, NIV). The nation of Israel has a bright and blessed future, and Jeremiah invested in that future.

As God's people, are we putting our money where our mouth is?

TEN

JEREMIAH 34–39; 52

Contemporary Events and Eternal Truths

> *"A nation that cannot preserve itself ought to die, and it will die—die in the grasp of the evils it is too feeble to overthrow."*
>
> —Senator Morris Shepherd[1]

In spite of the long-suffering of God and the faithful ministry of God's prophets, the kingdom of Judah was about to die. It was a nation with a glorious heritage—laws given from heaven by Moses, a land conquered by Joshua, a kingdom established by David and made magnificent by Solomon, a people in whose midst Jehovah dwelt in a splendid temple—and yet that glorious heritage couldn't prevent Judah's shameful ruin at the hands of the idolatrous Babylonians. The end had come.

What caused Judah's slow decay and final collapse? The historian would point to their unwise politics, particularly depending on Egypt for help, and we can't deny that Judah's leaders made some stupid decisions. But behind their "unwise politics" was a more insidious reason: *The leaders really didn't believe the Word of God.* During the dramatic rise and fall of empires in that stormy era, Judah looked *around* for allies instead of looking *up* for divine assistance. Instead of repenting and turning to God, they hardened their hearts against the Word and trusted their own wisdom.

Jeremiah recorded a number of events in Judah's final days that prove we can't treat God's Word any way we please and get away with it.

1. God's Word dishonored (Jer. 34:1–35:19)

The year was 588 B.C. and Nebuchadnezzar's army was successfully conquering the kingdom of Judah. The last two fortified cities were about to fall: Lachish, twenty-three miles from Jerusalem, and Azekah, eighteen miles from Jerusalem (34:7). Not only did Nebuchadnezzar bring his own invincible Babylonian troops, but also he demanded that the vassal countries he'd conquered send their share of recruits. In a sense, the entire Near East was attacking God's chosen people (see Ps. 74).

The destiny of the king (vv. 1-7). God gave weak King Zedekiah another opportunity to repent and save the city and the temple from ruin, but he refused to listen. Jeremiah warned him that the royal family and the court officials would not escape judgment and that he would be taken captive to Babylon, where he would die in peace. One act of faith and courage would have saved the city from ruin and the people from slaughter, but Zedekiah was afraid of his counselors (38:1-6) and was only a pawn in their hands.

The treachery of the people (vv. 8-22). At one point during the siege, Zedekiah and the people made a covenant with the Lord in the temple (34:15) to free all the Jewish slaves. A calf was slain and then cut in half, and the priests, officers, and people walked between the halves as a sign that they would obey the terms of the covenant (vv. 18-19; Gen. 15:18). In so doing, they were agreeing to free their Jewish slaves or be willing to suffer what the calf had suffered.

According to the Law of Moses, a Jewish master had to free his Jewish slaves at the end of seven years of service (Ex. 21:1-11; Deut. 15:12-18). The Jews hadn't done this for years, and now they decided it was a good thing to do. Why? Perhaps they felt that God would honor their obedience and defeat the enemy in some miraculous way, as He had done for Hezekiah (Isa. 36–37). Instead of believing God's Word and submitting to Babylon, the Jews tried to bargain with the Lord and "bribe" Him into helping their cause.

Of course, there were probably some practical considerations behind this covenant. If the slaves were free, they'd have to care for themselves; their masters wouldn't have to feed them or care for them. Also freemen were more likely to want to fight the enemy and maintain their newfound freedom. Whatever the reason, the effects of the covenant didn't last very long, for when there was a lull in the siege and Nebuchadnezzar went off to confront the Egyptian army (Jer. 34:21-22; 37:5-11), the masters all forced their slaves back into servitude. The solemn covenant made in the temple meant nothing.

Before we condemn these dishonest masters too much, let's admit that God's people often make promises to the Lord when they're in tough times, only to repudiate them when things get better. In my pastoral ministry, I've heard more than one suffering saint on a hospital bed promise to be the best Christian in the church if only God would give healing, and when He granted the request, he or she immediately forgot Him.

Jeremiah took advantage of this event to preach a sermon about Judah's treachery against the Lord (34:12-22). God had set the Israelites free from Egyptian bondage and had made a covenant with them to be their God, but they broke the covenant and returned to idolatry. Now they broke the Law by enslaving their own people unjustly. By what they did in the temple and the way they treated their fellow Jews, they profaned the name of the Lord. They hadn't really proclaimed freedom to their slaves, but God would proclaim "freedom" to the nation—" 'freedom' to fall by the sword, plague, and famine" (v. 17, NIV). The prophet predicted a terrible death for all the treacherous people who had participated in the covenant, and his predictions came true (vv. 19-20).

The integrity of the Rechabites (35:1-19). This event occurred eighteen years earlier, during the reign of Jehoiakim (609–597 B.C.). Jeremiah probably put the account at this point in the book for the sake of contrast: The people of Judah dishonored the Lord by disobeying His Law, while the Rechabites honored their father by obeying his command.

The Rechabites were a clan of nomadic people loyal to their ancestor Jonadab (2 Kings 10:15-23), who commanded them not to live in houses, not to have farms or vineyards, and not to drink wine. They were related to Moses' father-in-law (Jud. 1:16; 4:11) and for over 250 years had composed a small "separatist" clan in the nation. Because of the Babylonian invasion, they had forsaken their tents and moved into Jerusalem.

God didn't ask Jeremiah to serve the Rechabites wine in order to tempt them, because God doesn't tempt us (James 1:13-15). This was another "action sermon" to give Jeremiah an opportunity to tell the leaders of Judah how unfaithful they had been to God's covenant. It wasn't wrong for the Jewish people to drink wine so long as they didn't get drunk, but it was wrong for the Rechabites to drink wine *because they had made a commitment not to drink it.* God didn't commend these men for their personal standards but for their faithfulness to their father's command.

The message to the nation was clear. If the command of a mere man, Jonadab, was respected and obeyed by his family for over two centuries, why didn't the people of Israel and Judah obey the command of Almighty God—a command that the prophets had repeated over and over again? If a family tradition was preserved with such dedication, why was the very Law of God treated with such disrespect? Obeying Jonadab's words had only a limited and temporal significance, but disobeying God's Word had eternal consequences!

How often God's people are put to shame by the devotion and discipline of people who don't even know the Lord but who are intensely loyal to their family, their religion, or their personal pursuits. Even people who want nothing to do with the Word of God can be loyal to traditions and man-made codes. If Christians were putting into their spiritual walk the kind of discipline that athletes put into their chosen sport, the church would be pulsating with revival life.

2. God's Word protected (Jer. 36:1-32)

The fourth year of Jehoiakim was 605 B.C., the year of the fateful Battle of Carchemish when Pharaoh Necho defeated King Josiah and made Judah a vassal to Egypt (Jer. 46:2; 2 Chron. 35:20-27). Jehoiakim had gotten his throne only because Egypt had deposed his brother Jehoahaz. Jeremiah had been ministering for twenty-three years, and now God commanded him to write his messages in a scroll so they would be permanent and could be read by others. Note that his messages dealt with Israel, Judah, and all the nations, and when he wrote the second scroll, he added other material (Jer. 36:32). The first forty-five chapters of the Book of Jeremiah focus primarily on Israel and Judah, while chapters 45 to 51 deal with the other nations in the Near East.

God gives His Word (vv. 1-4, 17-18). This is what theologians call *inspiration*—that miraculous working of the Holy Spirit through a human writer so that what was written was the divine Word that God wanted recorded (2 Tim. 3:16;

2 Peter 1:20-21).[2] Inspiration is not some kind of "heavenly dictation," as though God completely bypassed the writer, for the authors of the various books of the Bible have their own distinctive styles and vocabularies. Without making him a robot, God guided Jeremiah in his choice of words; Jeremiah spoke these words to his secretary Baruch; and Baruch wrote them down in the scroll.

God declared His Word (vv. 5-26). Once again, God used human instruments to proclaim His Word to the people. "How shall they hear without a preacher?" (Rom. 10:14) Since Jeremiah wasn't allowed to go to the temple, he sent Baruch in his place. Baruch waited for a day when there would be a good crowd in the temple; when a fast was proclaimed several months later, probably because of the Babylonian menace, he took advantage of it.

It's interesting to see how different people responded to the Word of God. There were three public readings of the book, and the first one was to the people in the temple (Jer. 36:10). There's no record that the crowd responded in any special way. One man, Micaiah, however, became concerned because of what he had heard (v. 11). He was the grandson of Shaphan, the man who read the newly found book of the Law to King Josiah (2 Kings 22), so it's no wonder he had an interest in God's Word.

Micaiah told the princes about the book, and they asked to hear it, so Baruch read it to them (Jer. 36:12-19). Along with Micaiah, the officials trembled when they heard the Word (v. 16), for they knew that the nation was in great danger. They hid the scroll, told Baruch and Jeremiah to hide, and then went to report to the king that he needed to hear what Jeremiah had written.

The third reading of the scroll was before the king (vv. 21 26) and was done by Jehudi, who may have been one of the scribes. The king treated God's Word like fuel for the fire!

In spite of the remonstrances of three of his officials, the king continued cutting and burning the scroll until it was completely destroyed. The royal attendants who also heard the reading of the scroll showed no fear and thereby encouraged Jehoiakim in his evil deed.

Over the centuries, God's enemies have tried to destroy the Word of God but have always failed. They forget what Jesus said about the Word: "Heaven and earth shall pass away, but My words shall not pass away" (Matt. 24:35). "The grass withers and the flowers fall, but the word of our God stands forever" (Isa. 40:8, NIV; quoted in 1 Peter 1:25). Translators and preachers of the Word have been persecuted and martyred, but the truth of God still stands.

God preserves His Word (vv. 27-32). Any king who thinks he can silence God with a knife and a fire has a very high opinion of himself and a very low opinion of God. The Lord simply told Jeremiah to write another scroll, to which He added more material, including a special judgment on King Jehoiakim (Jer. 36:27-32). The same God who gives the Word has the power to protect and preserve the Word. The king had tried to destroy the Word, but the Word destroyed him!

King Jehoiakim and his officials would be punished for the disrespect they showed to the divine Word of God. The king would have no dynasty, nor would he have the burial of a king. His son Jehoiachin succeeded him and ruled for only three months, and then Jehoiakim's brother Zedekiah was made king. If the king and his flattering, servile officers had only feared the Word and obeyed it, they would have saved their nation suffering and ruin, but they preferred to go their own way and ignore God's voice.

3. God's Word rejected (Jer. 37:1–38:28)

"There's no problem so big or complicated that it can't be run away from." So read a piece of graffito found on a London wall in 1979, probably adapted from the "Peanuts" comic strip drawn by Charles Schulz. Whatever the source, the statement certainly represents King Zedekiah's approach to the terrible problems in Judah when the enemy was at the gates.

Next to Pontius Pilate (John 18–19), no ruler in Scripture reveals such indecision and vacillation as does King Zedekiah. These two chapters record four occasions when Zedekiah made contact with Jeremiah but rejected the Word that the prophet gave him. Listen to his feeble words.

"Pray for us!" (vv. 1-10) Afraid to come personally lest he lose the support of his officials, the king sent Jehucal (Jucal) and Zephaniah to solicit the prayers of Jeremiah for the king and the nation. Jehucal was not Jeremiah's friend, and he eventually urged the king to have the prophet killed (Jer. 38:1, 4). God had told Jeremiah not to pray for the people, but when the Babylonian army departed to deal with the Egyptians, it seemed like prayer wasn't needed (37:5-10). No doubt the false prophets announced that this event was a miracle, like the slaying of the Assyrian army in Hezekiah's day (Isa. 36–37). Once again, they were living on false hopes even though Jeremiah told them that Nebuchadnezzar would return and finish the work God had given him to do.

"Is there any word from the Lord?" (vv. 11-21) Until now, Jeremiah was a free man (v. 4), but his enemies found reason to imprison him. During the lull in the siege, Jeremiah tried to go home to Anathoth to take care of some family business, but the guard at the gate arrested him for defecting to the enemy. Of course, Jeremiah had preached surrender to Babylon (21:9) and would preach it again (38:2, 19; 39:9), but he certainly wasn't a traitor. He loved his nation and gave his life to try to save it, but his first loyalty was to the Lord.

Jeremiah was beaten and put into prison. When Zedekiah heard about it, he recognized it as an opportunity to talk safely to Jeremiah, for the officers would think the king was looking into Jeremiah's case. After bringing him to the palace, the king asked, "Is there any word from the Lord?" The prophet gave him an immediate answer, "Yes . . . you will be handed over to the king of Babylon" (37:17, NIV). Why say more? Jeremiah had already declared God's message many times, only to see the message rejected.

Jeremiah took the opportunity to expose the deceptive, optimistic messages of the false prophets. If they had been speaking the truth, the king should have asked them for a message from the Lord! Meanwhile, Jeremiah asked to be delivered from prison, a request that Zedekiah granted. The prophet was placed in the court of the prison and granted a daily ration of bread as long as the supply lasted. While we appreciate Zedekiah's concern to save Jeremiah, we wonder why the king didn't have a concern to save his people. He was afraid to change his policies because he was afraid of his advisers and officers.

"He is in Your hands" (38:1-13). Angry because Jeremiah's words were hurting the war effort, four of Zedekiah's officials banded together to urge the king to kill the prophet. We know nothing about Shephatiah. If Gedaliah was the son of the Pashur who had put Jeremiah in the stocks (20:1-6), he was certainly no friend to Jeremiah or to the truth. Jucal we met before (37:3); he may have been related to the guard who arrested Jeremiah (v. 13).[3] This Pashur must not be confused with the Pashur mentioned in Jeremiah 20. They accused Jeremiah of not seeking the welfare of the people, and yet the welfare of the people was the thing to which he had dedicated his life!

Too weak to oppose his own princes, the king gave in to their request. Instead of simply having Jeremiah slain, which would have been shedding innocent blood, the men had him imprisoned in an old cistern, where he sank in the mire at the bottom. The officers hoped that the prophet would eventually be forgotten there and would die. God, however, raised up a deliverer in the person of Ebed-Melech—a man from an alien race, who became an Old Testament "Good Samaritan."

The vacillating, spineless king usually agreed with the last person who spoke to him, and Ebed-Melech took advantage of that fault. Thus, the king gave Ebed-Melech permission to rescue Jeremiah. It wouldn't have taken thirty men to lift the prophet out of the cistern, but the king probably wanted to protect both his officer and the prophet from any attacks by Jeremiah's enemies. (Some commentators suggest that the text should read "three men." Thirty men would certainly call attention to themselves and what they were doing.)

Later, Jeremiah sent a special message of encouragement to Ebed-Melech (39:15-18)—that he would be delivered when the city was taken and that God would spare his life.

"Hide nothing from me" (vv. 14-28). As far as the record is concerned, this was the fourth and last contact King Zedekiah had with Jeremiah before the city fell to the Babylonians. His request presented Jeremiah with a dilemma: If Jeremiah told him the truth, the king might kill him, and he wouldn't obey the Word of God anyway! God gave the king one last chance to repent, but he only made excuses. If he surrendered to Nebuchadnezzar, he might be accused and abused by the Jews who had gone over to the enemy, and what would happen to his family left in the city? Perhaps the men who wanted to kill Jeremiah would kill them.

Jeremiah assured the king that if he obeyed the Word of the Lord, God would protect him and the city. But if he disobeyed, even the women in the palace would taunt him before the Babylonians (38:21-23). We can appreciate the king's concern for his wives and children, but the best way to protect them was to obey the will of God.

Still afraid of his own officers, the king told Jeremiah to

keep their conversation confidential. There's no suggestion that Jeremiah lied to the officers who questioned him. To begin with, we may not have a transcript of the complete conversation between Jeremiah and Zedekiah, and Jeremiah may have asked not to be returned to the house of Jonathan. Certainly in their second conversation, Jeremiah had made such a request (37:17-21). He was under no obligation to report everything to the officers, and he didn't have to lie in order to keep the conversation confidential.

Sometimes God judges a sinful nation by sending them weak leaders who are hesitant and vacillating and whose leadership (or lack of it) plunges the nation only deeper into trouble. "I will give children to be their princes, and babes shall rule over them" (Isa. 3:4, NKJV). The late John F. Kennedy put it this way: "We, the people, are the boss, and we get the kind of political leadership, be it good or bad, that we demand and deserve."[4] But Judah wasn't a democracy; the people didn't vote on their king. It was God who gave them what they deserved.

4. God's Word fulfilled (Jer. 39; 52)

These two chapters, along with 2 Kings 25 and 2 Chronicles 36, describe the tragic fall of Jerusalem, its plunder, and its destruction, as well as the Captivity and deportation of thousands of Jewish people. None of these things would have happened if only one of the kings had sincerely repented, trusted the Lord, and surrendered to the Babylonians.

God's judgment on Zedekiah (39:1-7; 52:1-11). The siege had begun on January 15, 588 (Jer. 52:4); and two and a half years later, on July 18, 586, the Babylonian army penetrated the city walls. The princes of Babylon set up their thrones in the Middle Gate and began to take over the reins of government. The "times of the Gentiles" had begun on God's prophetic calendar (Luke 21:24). When that period ends, the

Messiah will return to rescue His people and fulfill the promises made by the prophets.

Zedekiah, his family, and his staff tried to escape (see Jer. 34:3; Ezek. 12:1-12), but the Babylonians caught up with them and delivered them to Nebuchadnezzar at his headquarters at Riblah, some 200 miles north of Jerusalem. There he passed judgment on all of them, and the Babylonians were not known for their tenderness. He slaughtered Zedekiah's sons and then put out Zedekiah's eyes. Thus, the king's last visual memories would haunt him. Ezekiel had prophesied that Zedekiah would not see the land of Babylon (Ezek. 12:13), and his prophecy proved true. The king was bound and taken captive to Babylon, where he died.

God's judgment on the city (39:8-10; 52:12-34). "For this city has been to Me a provocation of My anger and My fury from the day that they built it, even to this day; so I will remove it from before My face" (Jer. 32:31, NKJV). Throughout his ministry, Jeremiah had warned the people that Jerusalem would be captured and destroyed (6:6; 19:8-9, 11-12, 15; 21:10; 26:6, 11; 27:17).

At the same time, the Babylonians pillaged the city and took the precious things out of the temple and carried them to Babylon. The soldiers rounded up the best of the people and took them to Babylon. There had been a previous deportation in 597 (52:28), and there would be a third deportation in 582 (52:30). The poorer, unskilled people were left to till the land. After all, somebody had to feed the soldiers who were left behind.

God's care for His servant (39:11-14). Since the Lord had promised that Jeremiah would survive all the opposition and persecution against him (1:17-19; 15:20-21), He moved upon Nebuchadnezzar to release the prophet and treat him kindly.[5] He was committed to Gedaliah, who later was named governor of the land (40:7). (This Gedaliah was not the one who wanted to kill Jeremiah, 38:1.)

I close with a solemn word from G. Campbell Morgan: "We in our security need to be reminded that for us also there may come the eleventh year, and the fourth month, and the tenth day of the month, when God will hurl us from our place of privilege, as He surely will, unless we are true to Him."[6]

ELEVEN

JEREMIAH 40–45

Tragedy Follows Tragedy

"Life only demands from you the strength you possess. Only one feat is possible—not to have run away."
—Dag Hammarskjold[1]

It's been said by more than one scholar that the one thing we learn from history is that we *don't* learn from history. This was certainly true of the destitute Jewish remnant in Judah after the fall of Jerusalem. Instead of seeking the Lord and making a new beginning, the remnant repeated the very sins that had led to the collapse of the nation and the destruction of the city: They wouldn't listen to the Word; they turned to Egypt for help; and they worshiped idols.

The sinful behavior of the people must have broken Jeremiah's heart, but he stayed with them and tried to get them to obey the Word of the Lord. God had punished the nation, but even this severe punishment didn't change their hearts. They were still bent on doing evil.

The drama was a tragic one with a cast of characters that is seen in every age. The script of history may change a bit from time to time, but the characters are still the same.

1. Jeremiah, the faithful shepherd (Jer. 40:1-6)
Jeremiah was given his freedom after the Babylonians captured Jerusalem (39:11-14), but somehow he got mixed in with the captives who were being readied at Ramah for their long march to Babylon. He was released and given the choice of going to Babylon and being cared for by the king or remaining in the land to care for the people. Being a man with a shepherd's heart, Jeremiah chose to dwell among the people (v. 14; 40:5-6).

The Babylonian captain of the guard preached a sermon that sounded a great deal like what Jeremiah had been saying for forty years! It must have been embarrassing for the Jews to hear a pagan Babylonian tell them they were sinners, but he was right in what he said. As God's people, we have to bow in shame when the world publicly announces the sins of the saints (Gen. 12:10-20; 20:1ff; 2 Sam. 12:14).

Jeremiah chose to join Gedaliah, whom Nebuchadnezzar had appointed governor of the land. Had the people followed the prophet and the governor, the Jewish remnant could have led safe and fairly comfortable lives even in the midst of ruin, but they chose not to obey. Even a severe chastening like the one Babylon brought to Judah didn't change their hearts, for the human heart can be changed only by the grace of God.

Was Jeremiah violating his own message when he remained with the people in the land? (24:4-10) Why stay with the "bad figs" when the future lay with the "good figs" who had been taken off to Babylon? Certainly Jeremiah knew how to discern the will of God, and the Lord knew how much the prophet loved the land and its people. Ezekiel was taken to Babylon in 597 and would start his ministry five years later (Ezek. 1:1-2), and Daniel had been taken there in 605. There were prophets to minister to the exiles, and Jeremiah was right to remain with the people in the land.

Jeremiah made difficult choices at the beginning and the

end of his ministry. It would have been much easier to serve as a priest, but he obeyed God's call to be a prophet, and it would have been much more comfortable in Babylon, but he opted to remain in the land of his fathers. Jeremiah was a true shepherd and not a hireling (see John 10:12-13).

2. Ishmael, a deceitful traitor (Jer. 40:7–41:18)

When the good news got out that Gedaliah was in charge of affairs in Judah, the people who had fled and hidden because of the siege began to come back to the land (Jer. 40:7, 11-12). Gedaliah was a good man from a good family, although events proved that he was very naive about practical politics.

The faithful governor (vv. 7-12). Gedaliah told the people exactly what Jeremiah had been telling them for many years: Serve the Babylonians and you will live safely in the land. The people couldn't reap any harvest of grain because the fields hadn't been sown during the siege, but they could gather the produce that had not been destroyed in the war. The remnant in Judah had to follow the same instructions that Jeremiah gave to the exiles in Babylon: Live normal lives, turn to the Lord with all your hearts, and wait for the Lord to deliver you (29:4-14). God had promised a future for the nation because the nation had important work to do.

The concerned captain (vv. 13-16). Johanan started out as a courageous leader, but later he led the people astray. We don't know how he and his associates heard about Ishmael's plot to assassinate Gedaliah, but their information was certainly accurate. Had Gedaliah listened to them, the governor's life would have been spared.

Why did Ishmael want to kill Gedaliah? The fact that the king of the Ammonites had hired him (40:14) suggests that he was making money, but much more was involved. The Ammonites had been a part of the "summit conference" in Jerusalem, where the nations allied with Judah had planned to break the Babylonian yoke (27:1-3). As a friend of Zedekiah and the king of Ammon, Ishmael didn't want to see the Jewish people submit to Nebuchadnezzar even after the war had ended. He was a patriot who used his patriotism to promote his own selfish purposes.

Perhaps the key factor had to do with pride and selfish ambition. Ishmael was a descendant of David through Elishama (41:1; 2 Sam. 5:16), and he no doubt felt that he should have been named ruler of the nation because of his royal blood. Who was Gedaliah that he should take the place of a king? The way the Babylonians had treated Ishmael's relative, King Zedekiah, was no encouragement to submit to their authority.

Johanan wanted to kill Ishmael, but Gedaliah refused the offer. In this, the governor was right, but he was wrong in not assembling a group of loyal men who could guard him day and night. Not only would that have told Ishmael that the governor knew what was going on, but also it would have protected Gedaliah's life from those who wanted to destroy him. The governor should have listened to Johanan and not been so naive about Ishmael. "For lack of guidance a nation falls, but many advisers make victory sure" (Prov. 11:14, NIV).

The deceitful murderer (41:1-18). In the Near East, when people eat together, they're pledging their friendship and loyalty to one another. Ishmael, however, used the meal as a trap to catch Gedaliah and his men so he could kill them. We don't know how many men were with the governor, but ten of Ishmael's men were able to dispatch them quickly.

To his terrible breach of hospitality he added hypocrisy, weeping before the eighty Jewish pilgrims who had come to worship, and then killing seventy of them. His greed was revealed when he spared the other ten in order to find out where their supply of food was hidden. He was a cunning and ruthless man who would stop at nothing to get his own way.

Ishmael climaxed his crimes by kidnapping the helpless Jewish remnant and starting for the land of the Ammonites. At this point, however, Johanan came to the rescue and delivered the remnant from Ishmael's power, but Ishmael escaped. It was a series of tragedies that probably could have been averted had Gedaliah listened to his friends and acted with more caution.

Johanan showed courage in rescuing the Jews, but when he was finally in charge, he revealed his own lack of faith by *wanting to take the remnant to Egypt!* He didn't remember the counsel of Gedaliah (Jer. 40:9) or the messages of Jeremiah, both of whom warned the Jews to stay in the land and not go to Egypt. How easy it is for a good man to go astray simply by turning away from the Word of God!

3. Johanan: a hypocritical leader (Jer. 42:1–43:13)

Johanan was once brave enough to want to kill Ishmael, but now he didn't have the courage to stand for what he knew was right. He was afraid to trust the Lord and stay in the land of Judah, perhaps because he feared what the Babylonians might do when they found out that Gedaliah was dead and Ishmael had filled a pit with dead bodies.

The insincere request (vv. 1-6). Their request to Jeremiah sounded sincere and spiritual, but there was deception in the hearts of the leaders, including Johanan (see 42:19-22). They had their minds already made up to go to Egypt, and they were hoping Jeremiah would agree with them. Sometimes God's people take this false approach in discerning the will of God. Instead of honestly seeking God's will, they go from counselor to counselor, asking for advice and hoping they'll find somebody who will agree with their hidden agenda.

The divine answer (vv. 7-22). The Lord kept the people waiting for ten days, possibly to give them time to search their hearts and confess their sins. During those ten days, they could see that the Lord was caring for them and that they had nothing to fear. That should have convinced them that the plan to flee to Egypt was a foolish one.

There were three parts to the answer Jeremiah gave them. First, he gave them *a promise (vv. 7-12).* He told them if they stayed in the land, God would build them and plant them (see 1:10). The prophet encouraged them not to be afraid of the Babylonians because the Lord was with the remnant and would care for them. It was God who was in charge, not the king of Babylon. Indeed, the day would come when this small remnant would be able to reclaim their lost lands and start to enjoy normal lives again.

The second part of Jeremiah's message was *a warning (42:13-18).* Ever since Abraham's lapse of faith in going to Egypt (Gen. 12:10-20), the Jews had a tendency to follow his example. Several times during the wilderness years, whenever they had a trial or testing, the Israelites talked of going back to Egypt. In fact, this was their cry at Kadesh-Barnea when they refused to enter the Promised Land (Num. 13–14). During the final years of the kingdom of Judah, there was a strong pro-Egyptian party in the government, because Egypt seemed to be the closest and strongest ally.

The prophet warned them against going to Egypt, where they thought they would enjoy peace, plenty, and security. The terrors they were trying to avoid in Judah would only follow them to Egypt, and the very judgments that God had sent against Judah during the siege would come upon them in the land of Pharaoh. God knew that Nebuchadnezzar would enter Egypt and punish the land, which he did in 568–567 B.C. (see Jer. 46:13-19).

Jeremiah ended his address with *an exposure of their hearts (vv. 19-22).* He announced publicly that they had tried to deceive him when they promised to obey the Lord's commands (42:5-6). They really didn't want either his prayers or

God's plans, they wanted the Lord to approve what they had already decided to do. But this was a fatal decision on their part, for if they carried out their plans, they would die in Egypt.

This event is a warning to us not to be insincere as we seek the will of God. In my itinerant ministry, I've frequently met people who wanted my counsel, and when I asked them if they had talked with their own pastor, the answer was often "Well, no, but he really doesn't know me or understand me."

"But I'm a total stranger to you!" I'd reply.

"Yes, but you seem to understand things better." Flattery!

My conviction is that these people have gone from one speaker to another, looking for somebody who will agree with what they already want to do. When they find him, they'll let their pastor know that "a man of God" gave them wise counsel. It's the Johanan syndrome all over again.

The arrogant rebellion (43:1-7). Convinced that God was wrong and they were right, Johanan and his friends so much as told Jeremiah he was a liar and a false prophet, and that God had neither sent him nor spoken to him. What a heartache it must have been for Jeremiah to hear such false accusations from his own people for whom he had suffered so much. In spite of all he had done for his people, Jeremiah was now accused of being like the false prophets whose lies had led the nation into ruin. Johanan even accused Baruch of influencing Jeremiah, although it's difficult to understand what kind of special power Baruch could possibly have had over this courageous prophet. But they had to blame somebody.

"So they came into the land of Egypt" (43:7). Once again, God's people walked by sight and not by faith.

The timely warning (vv. 8-13). This is Jeremiah's final "action sermon." While the Jews were watching, he gathered some large stones and set them in the clay (or mortar) before Pharaoh's house in Tahpanhes. Then he announced that Nebuchadnezzar's throne would one day sit on those stones while the king of Babylon passed judgment on the people. As he did to the temple in Jerusalem, so Nebuchadnezzar would do to the gods and temples in Egypt. His victory would be so easy that it would be like a shepherd wrapping his garment around himself! *And yet these are the very gods that the Jews would worship in Egypt, gods destined to be destroyed!*

4. The Jewish remnant: doomed idolaters (Jer. 44:1-30)

This is Jeremiah's last recorded message to his people, given in Egypt probably in the year 580. If he was called by God in 626, the thirteenth year of Josiah's reign (1:2), then he had been ministering forty-six years. You can't help admiring Jeremiah for his faithfulness in spite of all the discouragements that had come to his life.

A scathing indictment (vv. 1-14). No sooner did the Jewish remnant arrive in Egypt than they began to worship the local gods and goddesses, of which there were many. Jeremiah reminded them of *what they had seen* in the Lord's judgment on Judah (44:2-3). It was because of their idolatry that He had destroyed their land, the city of Jerusalem, and the temple. Then he reminded them of *what they had heard*—the messages of the prophets God had sent to rebuke them time after time (vv. 4-6).

But they hadn't learned their lesson, and now they were jeopardizing their future and inviting the wrath of God by repeating in Egypt the sins they'd committed in Judah. Had they forgotten the past? Were they unconcerned about their future? Didn't they realize that God could judge them in Egypt as easily as He had judged them in their own land? No wonder God called the Jews in the land "bad figs that nobody could eat." The future would rest with the exiles in Babylon who would one day return to their land and carry on the work God had given them to do.

A senseless argument (vv. 15-19). The men and women listening to Jeremiah tried to defend their sins by appealing to experience. They used the pragmatic argument: "If it works, it must be right." When they lived in Judah and secretly worshiped the Queen of Heaven (Astarte or Ishtar, goddess of fertility), everything went well with them. They had plenty of food and enjoyed comfortable circumstances. But when King Josiah made the people give up their idols, things began to get worse for them. Conclusion: They were better off when they disobeyed God and worshiped idols!

It seems that the women led the way in practicing idolatry, and their husbands cooperated with them. The women made vows to worship Astarte, *and their husbands approved of what they did (vv. 24-26).* According to Jewish law, if the husband approved his wife's vow, it was valid (Num. 30). Consequently, the wives blamed their husbands, and the husbands told Jeremiah that they didn't care what he said! They were going to worship Astarte just as they had done in Judah and in that way be sure things would go right for them.

A terrible pronouncement (vv. 20-30). How tragic that twice in a few short years, the Lord had to pronounce judgment on His people for the same sins! Jeremiah told them, "Go ahead then, do what you promised! Keep your vows! But hear the Word of the Lord" (Jer. 44:25-26, NIV). The Jews in Egypt would perish, and only a remnant of the remnant would ever return to their own land.

Jeremiah gave them a sign: Pharaoh Hophra, whom they were trusting to care for them, would be handed over to his enemies just as King Zedekiah was handed over to Nebuchadnezzar. Keep in mind that it was Pharaoh Hophra who agreed to help Zedekiah against the Babylonians, and his help proved worthless. Historians tell us that a part of the Egyptian army revolted against Hophra, and the general who stopped the rebellion was proclaimed king. He reigned along with Hophra, but three years later Hophra was executed.

Nebuchadnezzar then appeared on the scene, and Jeremiah's other prophecy was fulfilled.

It's likely that Jeremiah was dead when all this happened, but did the Jews in Egypt remember his words and take them to heart? Did they realize that he had faithfully declared God's Word and that what he had said was true? Did they repent and seek to obey?

5. Baruch: a faithful servant (Jer. 45:1-5)

Chronologically, this chapter belongs with Jeremiah 36, but it was placed here to perform several functions.

To begin with, this chapter introduces the prophecies in chapters 46–51, prophecies Baruch had written at Jeremiah's dictation in 605 B.C. Note in Jeremiah 25 the emphasis on Jeremiah's prophecies about the nations, and that this chapter was written at the same time as chapter 45, the fourth year of Jehoiakim. Most of the nations dealt with in chapters 46–51 are named in Jeremiah 25:15-26.

Second, Jeremiah 45 gives us insight into the man Baruch. As we noted earlier, he had a brother on the king's official staff who probably could have secured a good job for him in the palace. Instead, Baruch chose to identify with Jeremiah and do the will of God. We thank God for all that Jeremiah did, but we should also thank God for the assistance Baruch gave Jeremiah so the prophet could do his work. Moses had his seventy elders; David had his mighty men; Jesus had His disciples; Paul had his helpers, such as Timothy, Titus, and Silas; and Jeremiah had his faithful secretary.

Not everybody is called to be a prophet or apostle, but all of us can do the will of God by helping others do their work. Baruch was what we'd today call a "layman." Yet he helped a prophet write the Word of God. In my own ministry, I've appreciated the labors of faithful secretaries and assistants who have helped me in myriads of ways. I may have been on the platform, but without their assistance behind the scenes, I could never have gotten my work done. Baruch was willing to stay in the background and serve God by serving Jeremiah.

A third lesson emerges: Even the most devoted servants occasionally get discouraged. Baruch came to a point in his life where he was so depressed that he wanted to quit. "Woe is me now! For the Lord has added grief to my sorrow. I fainted in my sighing, and I find no rest" (45:3, NKJV). Perhaps the persecution of Jeremiah recorded in chapter 26 was the cause of this anguish. Maybe Baruch was considering leaving Jeremiah and asking his brother for an easier job in the palace.

The Lord, however, had a word of encouragement for His servant. First, He cautioned him not to build his hopes on the future of Judah, because everything would be destroyed in the Babylonian siege. A "soft job" in the government would lead only to death or exile in Babylon. Then God gave him a word of assurance: his life would be spared, so he didn't have to fear the enemy. God was proving to Baruch the reality of a promise that would be written centuries later: "But seek first the kingdom of God and His righteousness, and all these things shall be added to you" (Matt. 6:33, NKJV).

When we're serving the Lord and His people, we never want to seek great things for ourselves. The only important thing is that God's work is accomplished and God's great name is glorified. John the Baptist put it succinctly: "He must increase, but I must decrease" (John 3:30).

A crisis doesn't "make a person"; a crisis reveals what a person is made of. The crisis that followed the destruction of Jerusalem was like a goldsmith's furnace that revealed the dross as well as the pure gold. It's too bad there wasn't more gold.

How will you and I respond when "the fiery trial" comes? (1 Peter 4:12-19) I hope that, like Job, we'll come forth pure gold (Job 23:10).

TWELVE

JEREMIAH 46–49

God Speaks to the Nations

"I have lived, Sir, a long time, and the longer I live, the more convincing proofs I see of this truth—that God governs in the affairs of men."

—Benjamin Franklin[1]

Jeremiah had spoken to his people for over forty years, but they wouldn't listen; now he spoke to the nations related in some way to the Jewish people. As God's spokesman, Jeremiah was "handing the cup" to these nations (25:15ff) and declaring what God had planned for them. He was called to be "a prophet unto the nations" (1:5), and he was fulfilling his ministry.

While these names, places, and events are ancient history to most of us, the lessons behind these events reveal to us the hand of God in the rise and fall of rulers and nations. One of the repeated phrases in these chapters is God's "I will," for "history is His story," as A.T. Pierson used to say. You will also note that God judged *the gods of these nations,* just as He had judged the gods of Egypt before Israel's Exodus (Ex. 12:12).

1. Judgment on Egypt (Jer. 46:1-28)

Pharaoh Necho had defeated Judah and killed King Josiah at Megiddo in 609 (2 Chron. 35:20-27), but then Nebuchadnezzar defeated Necho at the famous Battle of Carchemish in 605, the fourth year of Jehoiakim. That defeat broke the power of Egypt and made Babylon supreme in the Near East. Jeremiah described the battle from Egypt's viewpoint (Jer. 46:3-12); then he described Babylon's invasion of Egypt (vv. 13-26), concluding with an application to the people of Israel (vv. 27-28).

Egypt's shameful defeat (vv. 3-12). Jeremiah wrote a graphic description of the famous Battle of Carchemish. He described the officers confidently preparing their troops (vv. 3-4) and then watching the soldiers flee in terror before the Babylonian army (vv. 5-6). Jeremiah doesn't even describe the battle! The phrase "fear was round about" is the familiar "terror on every side" that we've met before (6:25; 20:3) and will meet again (49:29).

When the Egyptian army approached the battlefield, they looked like the Nile in flood season (46:8a). The military leaders were sure of victory (v. 8b), and their mercenaries were eager to fight (v. 9), but the Lord had determined that Egypt would lose the battle. "That day belongs to the Lord, the Lord Almighty" (v. 10, NIV).[2] It was a "holy war" in that God offered Egypt as a sacrifice (v. 10). Egypt's wounds were incurable and her shame was inevitable (vv. 11-12).

Babylon's triumphant invasion (vv. 13-26). Historians tell us that this occurred in 568–67 and fulfilled not only this prophecy but also the "action sermon" Jeremiah had described earlier (43:8-13). Once again, the Egyptian army stood fast as the Babylonians swept down on them. Before long, however, the men not only fell over but also fell upon one another in their haste to escape (46:13-15). Their mercenaries cried, "Arise, and let us go again to our own people, and to the land of our nativity" (v. 16), and they deserted their posts.

The Babylonian soldiers called Pharaoh Necho "a big noise." We today would probably call him a "loudmouth" or "big mouth," because he was nothing but talk and hot air.[3] While Necho may have been only hot air, Nebuchadnezzar filled the horizon like a huge mountain when he appeared on the scene (v. 18).

Look at the graphic images Jeremiah used. Egypt was like a heifer (v. 20). The mercenaries in Pharaoh's army were like fatted calves that stampeded (v. 21), and the Egyptian soldiers fled like hissing serpents (v. 22) and fell before the Babylonians like trees before woodcutters (v. 23). The invading army was like a swarm of locusts that couldn't be avoided (v. 23). Alas, Egypt was like a young woman being violated and unable to escape (v. 24).

The defeat of Egypt was the defeat of Egypt's gods (v. 25). This didn't mean that the gods of Babylon were stronger than the gods of Egypt, for all of their gods were nothing. It meant that Jehovah had proved Himself stronger than the many gods of Egypt and Babylon by being in control of the entire battle. Nebuchadnezzar won and Pharaoh Necho lost because God decreed it. But God also decreed that Egypt would be restored (v. 26), a promise He also gave to Moab (48:47), Ammon (49:6), and Elam (v. 39).

Israel's assured future (vv. 27-28). They shouldn't have been there, but a band of Jews was in Egypt, and this invasion would affect them terribly. The remnant in Judah and the exiles in Babylon would hear of this victory and wonder whether anything on earth could stop Nebuchadnezzar. God had promised that the exiles would be released from Babylon in seventy years, but Babylon looked stronger than ever.

God's Word will stand no matter what the newspapers report! "I will save you," God promised. "I will wipe out the nations, but I won't wipe you out."[4] Twice the Lord said,

"Don't be afraid." No matter how dark the day, God always gives His people the bright light of His promises (2 Peter 1:19-21).

2. Judgment on Philistia (Jer. 47:1-7)

The Philistine people probably came from Crete (Caphtor, v. 4). They built a wealthy nation by developing a merchant marine that sailed the Mediterranean and acquired goods from many lands. But their destiny was destruction. Tyre and Sidon had been confederate with Judah in an attempt to stop Nebuchadnezzar (27:3).

This time Jeremiah used the image of the rising river to describe the Babylonian army as it flooded over the land (47:2). So terrible was the invasion that parents would flee for their lives and leave their children behind (v. 3; see 49:11). The people would act like mourners at a funeral (47:5) and ask the Lord when He would put up the terrible sword of His judgment (v. 6). But this sword would continue to devour the land until God's work of judgment was finished.

3. Judgment on Moab (Jer. 48:1-47)

The Moabites were descendants of Lot (Gen. 19:20-38) and, along with the Ammonites, the enemies of the Jews. During the Babylonian crisis, however, both Moab and Ammon allied themselves with Judah in an ill-fated attempt to defeat Nebuchadnezzar (Jer. 27:3). Over twenty different places are named in this chapter, some of which we can't identify with certainty, but the list shows how detailed God can be when He wants to predict future events.[5]

In 582, Nebuchadnezzar's army invaded Moab, destroyed the people and the cities, and left desolation behind. The reason for this judgment was Moab's pride (48:7, 29-30) and complacency (v. 11). The Moabites were certain that their god Chemosh would protect them (vv. 7, 13, 35, 46) and that no army could scale the heights to reach them on their secure plateau (v. 8).

The image in verses 11-13 pictures Moab as a self-satisfied nation, feeling very secure, like wine aging in a jar and becoming tastier. Because the nation had been comfortable and self-sufficient, they were unprepared for what happened. The Babylonians emptied the wine from jar to jar and then broke the jars! (See v. 38 for another broken jar image.) Instead of sitting on their mountainous throne, the nation had to come down and grovel on the parched earth (vv. 17-18). The horn and the arm are both symbols of strength (v. 25), but Moab's horn was cut off and her arm broken. She had no strength.

The wine image is picked up again in verses 26-27. The nation was drunk from the cup that God gave her (25:15-16, 27-29), and like someone at a drunken party, she was vomiting and wallowing in her own vomit. It isn't a pretty picture. The image then changes to that of a dove hiding in a cave, wondering what will happen next (48:28). The Babylonians are pictured as an eagle swooping down on its prey (v. 40; see Deut. 28:49; Ezek. 17:3); a dove is no match for an eagle.

The remarkable thing is that Jeremiah wept over the fall of Moab (Jer. 48:31) and lamented like a flutist at a funeral (vv. 36-38). Certainly his grief is evidence of the compassion God has for people who are destroyed because of their sins against the Lord. God has "no pleasure in the death of [the wicked]" (Ezek. 18:32; see 18:23; 33:11) and does all He can to call them to repentance before judgment falls.

There is no escape (Jer. 48:44-46; see Amos 5:19). Flee from the army, and you'll fall into a pit. Climb out of the pit, and you'll be caught in a trap. Escape from the trap, and you'll be engulfed by a fire. Escape from the fire, and you'll be captured and taken away to Babylon. Sinners need to face the fact that there is no place to hide when God begins to judge (Rev. 20:11-15). For lost sinners today, their only hope is faith in Jesus Christ, who died for the sins of the world. They need to flee for refuge to Christ (Heb. 6:18)—the only refuge for their souls.

After writing a long chapter on judgment, Jeremiah ended with a promise: "Yet will I bring again the Captivity [restore the fortunes] of Moab in the latter days" (Jer. 48:47). This statement refers to the future Kingdom Age when Jesus Christ will reign.

4. Judgment on Ammon (Jer. 49:1-6)

Like the Moabites, the Ammonites were the product of Lot's incestuous union with one of his daughters (Gen. 19:20-38) and the enemies of the Jews.

Jeremiah's first accusation is that the Ammonites moved into Israel's territory when Assyria took the Northern Kingdom captive in 722 B.C. The Ammonites took Gad and other cities, as though the Jews would never return. The phrase "their king" in Jeremiah 49:1 and 3 can be translated *Molech,* which is the name of the chief god of the Ammonites (1 Kings 11:5, 7, 33). They boasted that their god was stronger than the God of Israel, but one day Israel will "drive" the Ammonites out of the land (Jer. 49:2, NIV).

The Ammonites boasted that their fruitful valley was secure because mountains protected it on three sides (v. 4), but that couldn't stop the invasion. God had decreed judgment for proud Ammon, and nothing they trusted could prevent the invasion.

Once again, however, we see the goodness and mercy of the Lord in promising to restore the fortunes of the Ammonites when He restores the fortunes of Israel and Judah in the future kingdom. God restores them, not because of their own merits, but because they share in the glories that Israel will experience when King Jesus sits on David's throne. "Salvation is of the Jews" (John 4:22).

5. Judgment on Edom (Jer. 49:7-22)

The Edomites had descended from Jacob's elder brother Esau, whom God bypassed for the blessing, giving it to Jacob (Gen. 25:19-34; see Gen. 36). The Edomites weren't friendly to the Jews, but their common enemy, Babylon, caused Edom to join the "Jerusalem summit" in the days of Zedekiah (Jer. 27:3).

You will want to read the prophecy of Obadiah and see how the two prophets agree. Since we don't know when the Book of Obadiah was written, we aren't sure whether Jeremiah borrowed from Obadiah or vice versa. The prophets occasionally quoted one another, an evidence that the same God was the author of their messages. Furthermore, there are a number of parallels between Isaiah and Jeremiah.

Edom's judgment would be like a harvest where nothing would be left for the gleaners (49:9-10; Lev. 19:10; Deut. 24:21). God would do a thorough job the first time. Like the other nations, Edom would have to "drink of the cup" (Jer. 49:12) because of her pride and rebellion against the Lord (v. 16). With their cities in the rocks, such as Petra, they thought they were impregnable (vv. 16-18), but they would be destroyed like the cities of the plain, Sodom and Gomorrah (Gen. 19).

Nebuchadnezzar would come upon Edom like a lion bounding out of the thick growth around the Jordan River, and he wouldn't spare the flock (Jer. 49:19-21). He would come like an eagle and so frighten the Edomites that they would agonize like women in travail (v. 22; see 48:40-41). The people of Edom were noted for their great wisdom (49:7; Job 2:11), but they wouldn't be able to devise any plan that would save them from the invasion of the Babylonian army.

In the midst of wrath, the Lord remembers mercy (Hab. 3:2) and shows compassion for the widows and orphans (Jer. 49:11; see Ex. 22:21-24; 23:9; Lev. 19:33; Deut. 10:18; 27:19). But Edom's pride would bring her low, as pride always does.

6. Judgment on Syria [Damascus] (Jer. 49:23-27)

The Prophet Isaiah condemned Damascus, the capital of Syria (Isa. 17). Amos accused the Syrians of treating the people of Gilead like grain on a threshing floor (Amos 1:3-5). God would judge them for their inhumanity and brutality to His people.

According to Jeremiah, hearing the news of the approaching Babylonian army, the people of Damascus would become as troubled as the restless sea, as weak and shaky as a sick patient, and as full of pain as a woman in travail (Jer. 49:23-24). They would abandon their ancient cities and try to escape, but their best young men would be killed in the streets and their fortress would be burned to the ground.

This message is brief, but it carries power. How much does God have to say to convince people that His wrath is about to fall?

7. Judgment on Kedar and Hazor (Jer. 49:28-33)

These are two desert peoples. Kedar was related to Ishmael (Gen. 25:13). We aren't sure of the origin of Hazor, which is not to be confused with the city of that name in northern Palestine (Josh. 11).

These two nomadic Arab nations lived by raising sheep and camels. When Nebuchadnezzar attacked them in 599–598 B.C., however, they lost everything. Once again, we meet the phrase "fear is on every side" (Jer. 49:29; see 20:3). These two Arab nations were guilty of living at ease, isolating themselves from others, and manifesting pride and arrogant self-confidence (49:31). They didn't need God, and they didn't need the help of any other people! When Nebuchadnezzar arrived on the scene, they learned how foolish they had been.

8. Judgment on Elam (Jer. 49:34-39)

The Elamites were a Semitic people who were neighbors of the Babylonians. (Along with this paragraph, they are mentioned in Gen. 14:1; Isa. 11:11; 21:2; 22:6; Jer. 25:25; Ezek. 32:24; Dan. 8:2.) Their country was located beyond the Tigris River across from Babylon, and it eventually became part of the Medo-Persian Empire. God gave Jeremiah this prophecy about 597 B.C., during the reign of Zedekiah.

Since the Elamite soldiers were known for their archery, God promised to break their bows (Jer. 49:35). He compared the Babylonian army to a storm that would not only blow from all directions but also scatter the people in all directions (v. 36). Whenever a nation was defeated, the victors would set up their king's throne in the city gate (1:15; 39:3; 43:8-13), and that's what God promised to do in Elam (49:38). He would let them know that He was King.

The Lord ended this description of judgment with a promise of mercy. Why He chose to restore Egypt, Moab, Ammon, and Elam is not explained, but they will share in the kingdom because of God's grace.

As you studied these chapters, perhaps you became weary of reading the same message: Judgment is coming and there's no escape. There's a sameness about what God said about these nine nations; and if we aren't careful, that sameness can produce "tameness" and cause us to lose a heart sensitive to the Lord's message.

Keep in mind, however, that these prophecies were written about real men, women, and children, and that what Jeremiah wrote actually came true. Whole civilizations were wiped out because of their sins, and eventually Babylon itself was destroyed. This means that multitudes of people died and went into an eternity of darkness.

God sees what the nations do, and He rewards them justly. What King Hezekiah said about the Lord needs to be emphasized today: "O Lord Almighty, God of Israel, enthroned between the cherubim, You alone are God over all the kingdoms of the earth" (Isa. 37:16, NIV). Joshua called Him "the Lord of all the earth" (Josh. 3:11), and both Jesus and Paul called Him "Lord of heaven and earth" (Luke 10:21; Acts 17:24).

God never gave the Law of Moses to any of the nations that Jeremiah addressed, but He still held them accountable for the sins they committed against Him and against humanity. Because of the witness of creation around them and conscience within them, they were "without excuse" (Rom. 1:17-32, especially v. 20) and guilty before God.

In recent history, the nations haven't acted any better than the ones recorded in Jeremiah 46–49. Innocent blood is shed legally as millions of babies are aborted in their mother's wombs. International terrorism, genocide, exploitation of people and material resources, war, crime, the abuse of children, and a host of other sins have stained the hands of nations with blood. What will they do when the Judge becomes angry and starts to avenge the innocent?

"It is a fearful thing to fall into the hands of the living God" (Heb. 10:31).

THIRTEEN

JEREMIAH 50–51

Babylon Is Fallen!

"After all, we are not judged so much by how many sins we have committed but by how much light we have rejected."

—Vance Havner[1]

After declaring the destiny of the Gentile nations (Jer. 46–49), the prophet now focused on Judah's hateful enemy, the empire of Babylon. Jeremiah devoted 121 verses to the future of nine nations and 44 verses to the defeat and destruction of Jerusalem. When we count the number of verses in Jeremiah 50 and 51, however, he devoted 110 verses to the fall of Babylon. It is an important subject indeed!

In Scripture, the city of Babylon is contrasted to the city of Jerusalem—the proud city of man versus the holy city of God. In Hebrew, the name *babel* means "gate of God," but *babel* is so close to the word *balal* ("confusion") that it's associated with the famous tower of Babel and the confusion of human languages (Gen. 11:1-9). The founder of Babylon was Nimrod (10:10), "a mighty hunter before the Lord" (v. 9, NIV). Some students interpret this to mean "a mighty rebel against the Lord."[2] Babel/Babylon is a symbol of rebellion against God, the earthly city of human splendor opposing the heavenly city that glorifies God. All of this culminates in the Babylon of Revelation 17:1–19:10, "Babylon the Great" that symbolizes the anti-God system that controls the world in the end times and then is destroyed by the Lord. There are many parallels between Jeremiah 50–51 and Revelation 17–18, and I suggest you read all four chapters carefully.

Jeremiah wrote this prophecy during the fourth year of Zedekiah (594–93) and gave the scroll to Baruch's brother Seraiah to read in Babylon and then throw into the Euphrates (Jer. 51:59-64). Since Seraiah was an officer in Zedekiah's cabinet, he had access to things officially diplomatic. This would have been the last of Jeremiah's "action sermons," performed without Jeremiah, symbolizing the complete destruction of the great Babylonian Empire.

Jeremiah 50–51 is something like an extended declaration coupled with a conversation. Usually it's the Lord speaking through His prophet, but occasionally we hear the Jewish people speaking and the Lord answering them. God speaks to and about Babylon; He also speaks to the invading army; and He speaks to the exiles of Judah. Three movements are in this declaration: God declares war on Babylon (50:1-28); God assembles the armies against Babylon (50:29–51:26); and God announces victory over Babylon (vv. 27-58).

Jeremiah's prophecy about Babylon has both a near and a far fulfillment. The Medes and Persians captured Babylon in 539 (see Dan. 5), but they didn't destroy the city. Cyrus issued a decree that the Jews could return to their land (Ezra 1:1-4), which many of them did in three stages: in 538 (Ezra 1–6), 458 (Ezra 7–10) and 444 (Book of Nehemiah). It was Alexander the Great who finally destroyed Babylon in

330 and left it a heap of ruins. Since Babylon symbolizes the anti-God world system, however, the ultimate fulfillment is recorded in Revelation 17–18. Remember, the prophets often looked at "two horizons," one near and one far, as they spoke and wrote about the future.

1. God declares war on Babylon (Jer. 50:1-28)

"Announce and proclaim!" is the commandment. "Raise the signal!" God declared war on Babylon and announced that her great god Bel (also called Marduk) was about to be shamefully defeated.

God declared war on both Babylon and the gods of Babylon. The word translated "idols" means "wooden blocks," and the word translated "images" means "dung pellets." The Lord didn't think much of their gods! The invaders would come from the north just as Nebuchadnezzar came from the north to conquer Judah (1:11-15).

God speaks to and about the Jews (vv. 4-10). He saw them as lost sheep without a shepherd, a flock greatly abused both by their leaders and their captors. While the immediate application is to the return of the exiles from Babylon, the ultimate reference includes the gathering of the Jews in the latter days. God warned the people to flee from Babylon so as not to be caught in the judgment that would fall (Isa. 48:20; Rev. 18:4). He would bring the Medes and the Persians against Babylon and give them total victory.

God speaks to Babylon (vv. 11-13). Now we find out why God was destroying this great empire. To begin with, the Babylonians were glad that they could devastate and subjugate Judah. Yes, Babylon was God's tool to chasten His sinful people, but the Babylonians went too far and enjoyed it too much. They acted like a joyful calf threshing the grain and getting his fill! Any nation that cursed the Jews will ultimately be cursed by God (Gen. 12:1-3). As they treated Judah, so

God will treat them (see Jer. 51:24, 35, 49).

God speaks to the invading armies (vv. 14-16). Just as Babylon had been God's tool to chasten Judah, so the invaders (Cyrus with the Medes and Persians, and later Alexander with his Greek army) would be God's weapon to defeat Babylon. God spoke to the invading armies and commanded them to get their weapons ready and shout for victory, because they would win the battle. This was no ordinary war; this was "the vengeance of the Lord" (v. 15, NIV).

God speaks about the Jews (vv. 17-20). Once more Jeremiah used the image of the scattered flock. Assyria had ravaged Israel (the Northern Kingdom), and Babylon had ravaged Judah (the Southern Kingdom), but now God would punish Babylon as He had Assyria. (Assyria fell to a Babylonian-Median alliance in 609.) God will bring His people back to their own land, where the flock may graze safely and peacefully. The prophet then looked down to the latter days when God will wipe away the nation's sins and establish His New Covenant with them. We see the "two horizons" of prophecy again.

God speaks to the invaders (vv. 21-27). The Lord was in command of the invasion, and His orders were to be carried out explicitly. Babylon "the rod" (Isa. 10:5) was itself shattered. Babylon was caught in God's trap and couldn't escape God's weapons. Their fine young men would be slaughtered like cattle, for the day of judgment for Babylon had come.

The Jewish remnant speaks (v. 28). We hear the exiles who had fled the city and arrived in Judah as they report the fall of Babylon. The ultimate sin of the Babylonians was the burning of the temple, and for that sin the ultimate total destruction of their city was their punishment.

2. God gathers the armies against Babylon (50:29–51:26)

The first command had been "Declare among the nations!" But now the command was, "Call together the archers!" God ordered the armies of the Medes and Persians (and later the Greeks) to shoot to kill and allow no one to escape.

God speaks to Babylon (50:31–51:4). He told them that He was against them because of their pride (50:31-32) and because of the way they had made the Jews suffer unnecessarily (v. 33). The exiles couldn't free themselves, but their Strong Redeemer would free them! The phrase "plead their cause" speaks of a court case. Jehovah was defense attorney, judge, and jury, and He found Babylon guilty.

Now the Lord told Babylon what to expect on the day of their judgment. The first picture is that of a sword going through the land and cutting down the people (vv. 35-38). God's sword will even attack the waters and dry them up (v. 38). Why? Because "it is a land of idols" (v. 38, NIV) and God wanted to reveal that the idols were nothing. Like the overthrow of Sodom and Gomorrah, nothing will be left. Babylon will become a haven for animals and birds, and the city will never be restored.

The Lord directed the Babylonians' attention to the great army that He had called from the north—a cruel army without mercy, whose march sounded like the roaring of the sea (v. 42). This report paralyzed the king of Babylon. Like a hungry lion, looking for prey (see 49:19-21), Cyrus (and then Alexander) will attack Babylon, and nobody will be able to resist. God's chosen servant will always succeed. The Lord's judgment on Babylon will be like the winnowing of the grain: "Great Babylon" will be blown away like chaff along with its idols!

God speaks to the Jews (vv. 5-10). God assured His people that He hadn't forsaken ("widowed") them, and He ordered them a second time (50:8) to get out of Babylon when the opportunity arises. When Cyrus opened the door for them to go home, about 50,000 Jews returned to Judah to restore Jerusalem and the temple. Babylon had been a "winecup" (see 25:15) in God's hands, making the nations act like drunks (Rev. 18:3), but now the cup would be smashed and Babylon's power broken. "Wail for her!" (Jer. 51:8, NIV) finds a fulfillment in Revelation 18:9ff. Anybody who pinned their hope on Babylon was doomed to disappointment, but so is anyone today who pins his or her hope on this present world. "The world is passing away" (1 John 2:17, NKJV).

To whom does "we" in Jeremiah 51:9 refer—to the Jews or to Babylon's allies who deserted her? Since the "us" in verse 10 refers clearly to the Jews and their vindication, it is likely that the exiles are speaking in verse 9, because Jeremiah had instructed them to be a blessing while living in Babylon (29:4-14). No doubt many of the Jews did seek the Lord, confess their sins, and trust His promise of deliverance. Some of them certainly prepared their sons and daughters to return to the land. They had the truth about Jehovah God and would have shared it with their captors, but the Babylonians preferred to taunt the Jews instead of listen to them discuss their religion (Ps. 137).

God speaks to Babylon (vv. 11-23). He warned them to get their weapons ready, set up their standards on the walls, and post their watchmen, because the invasion was about to begin. "Your end has come, the time for you to be cut off" (Jer. 51:13, NIV). They had been weaving the luxurious tapestry of their power and wealth on the loom, but now God would cut it off and put an end to their plans (v. 13, NIV).[3]

The enemy soldiers would swoop down on the Babylonians like locusts and prove the utter helplessness of the gods of Babylon. Jeremiah revealed the stupidity of making and worshiping idols (vv. 15-19), and he magnified the greatness of the one true and living God (see 10:12-16; Isa. 40:12-26).

God speaks to His general (vv. 20-24).[4] Just as Assyria had been God's "rod" (Isa. 10:5-19), so His chosen commander (Cyrus, and later Alexander) would be His "hammer" to break the power of Babylon. The word "break" (shatter) is used nine times in this passage. They would pay Babylon back with the same treatment Nebuchadnezzar had given others. There is a law of compensation in God's working in history, and the Lord will enforce it.

God speaks to Babylon (vv. 25-26). The city of Babylon sat on a plain, but in the sight of the nations, it was a huge destroying mountain that loomed on the horizon of history. By the time God was through with it, however, Babylon would be nothing but an extinct volcano ("a burnt mountain," Jer. 51:25). Nobody would even excavate the ruins to find stones to build with; the city would be deserted and desolate forever.

3. God announces victory over Babylon (Jer. 51:27-58)

Throughout this prophecy, God has frequently announced the fall of Babylon, but this closing section seems to focus on God's total victory over the enemy.

God describes the victory (vv. 27-33). God's armies were prepared, the commanders were ready, and the battle began; but the Babylonian army was helpless! They lay on the walls exhausted; their courage had failed them. The city was in flames, and the bars of the gates were broken. Nothing kept the enemy from entering the city and doing to it what the Babylonians had done to Jerusalem.[5]

The Babylonians had an effective courier system and could quickly send messages to the various parts of their vast empire. In fact, Jeremiah described the runners meeting and exchanging messages for the king: "The river crossings have been seized!" "The marshes are set on fire!" "The soldiers are terrified!" "The city has been captured!" (see vv. 31-32, NIV) It was God's harvest, and Babylon was on the threshing floor.[6]

God speaks to the Jews (vv. 34-50). First, the Jews reminded the Lord what Nebuchadnezzar had done to them (vv. 34-35). Like a vicious monster, he had picked up Judah as if it were a jar filled with food, swallowed down the food, vomited it up, and then broken the jar! He had chewed them up and spit them out! Now the Jews wanted the Lord to repay the Babylonians for all the suffering they had caused the people of God.

God's reply was encouraging: Like a court advocate, He would take their case, plead their cause, and vindicate them (v. 36). The Lord described vividly what would happen to Babylon: The ruins of the city would become the haunt of animals and birds, a perpetual cemetery for the people slain in the invasion, a slaughter house where people would die like so many cattle, sheep, and goats.

Sheshach in verse 41 is a code name for Babylon (25:26), following a system where the last letter of the alphabet is substituted for the first, the next to the last for the second, and so on. Why Jeremiah used a code name for the enemy in one sentence and then the real name in the next sentence isn't easy to understand.

Nevertheless, the enemy army would cover Babylon just as the sea covers the land (51:42), but when "the tide is out," a desert will be left behind. The Babylonian "monster" may have swallowed up God's people, but the Lord would force it to disgorge them (v. 44), and the new king (Cyrus) would permit God's people to return home. "The wall of Babylon shall fall" (v. 44) literally came true under Alexander, but "the wall came down" when Cyrus decreed that the exiles could go back to Judah and rebuild their temple.

For the third time, God ordered His people to get out of Babylon (v. 45; see 50:8; 51:6) and not to linger (51:50; see Gen. 19:16). Neither should they be afraid of the rumors they would hear about, which were about to happen. They didn't need to be afraid of the vain Babylonian idols that could do nothing to hinder them. Heaven and earth will sing songs of praise when Babylon falls (Jer. 51:48; Rev. 18:20ff).

The Jews speak and God replies (vv. 51-58). The exiles felt disgraced before the world because of what the Babylonians had done to the temple in Jerusalem. If the Lord wasn't strong enough to protect His house, how could He ever be strong enough to defeat Babylon? If they left Babylon, they would go home only to ruin and shame. During the years of their captivity, those who had obeyed Jeremiah's instructions (Jer. 29:4-14) probably enjoyed fairly comfortable lives. Thus, they would be exchanging security for danger and plenty for want.[7]

God, however, made it clear that there was no future in Babylon, for He had determined to destroy the city. "For the Lord [is a] God of recompenses" (51:56). If His people remained in Babylon, they would suffer the fate of the city. If they obeyed the Lord and returned home, they would experience a new beginning under the blessing of the Lord.

It's a matter of walking by faith and not by sight, trusting God's Word instead of our own human evaluation. The exiles saw the high walls and huge gates of the city and concluded that such fortifications would repel any enemy, but they were wrong. Those walls and gates would become only "fuel for the flames" when the invaders arrived on the scene (v. 58, NIV).

"Babylon is fallen, is fallen, that great city!" (Rev. 14:8)

And Babylon is still fallen!

POSTLUDE

"Defeat doesn't finish a man—quitting does. A man is not finished when he's defeated. He's finished when he quits."

—Richard M. Nixon

Jeremiah died an old man, probably in Egypt, and like the grave of Moses, his burial place is a mystery. The brave prophet has long turned to dust, but the words that he wrote are still with us, because God's Word endures forever.

He wrote a long and difficult book, and we haven't been able to deal with everything he wrote. However, you can't help but glean from his life and ministry some clear and important lessons that apply to all of God's people today.

1. In difficult days, we need to hear and heed the Word of God. Since hindsight always has twenty-twenty vision, it's obvious to us that the leaders of Judah did a very stupid thing by resisting what Jeremiah told them to do. Judah had sinned its way into trouble and judgment, and they thought they could negotiate their way out, but it didn't work. What they needed was faith in God's Word and obedience to God's will. Had they confessed their sins, turned to God, and submitted to Nebuchadnezzar, they would have saved their lives, their temple, and their city.

2. True prophets of God are usually (if not always) persecuted. The civil and religious leaders of Judah preferred the pleasant messages of the false prophets to the strong words of God's true servant, because the human heart wants to rest, not repent. It wants peace, but it wants it without having to deal with the basic cause of unrest—unbelief.

The people of Israel resisted God's messengers and challenged their authority from the time of Moses to the days of the apostles. It's difficult to name a prophet or apostle who didn't suffer persecution. If Jeremiah showed up today at the United Nations or some senate or parliament, and spoke as he did to the leaders of Judah, he would probably be laughed at and thrown out. But it's a dangerous thing to be a "popular preacher" who has no enemies and pleases everybody. "Prophets are almost extinct in the religious world today," said Vance Havner. "The modern church is a 'non-prophet' organization."[1]

3. True patriotism isn't blind to sin. Charles Jefferson wrote:

> He [Jeremiah] loved his country so passionately he was willing to die for it as a traitor. He loved his country so intensely that he would not leave it even after Jerusalem was in ruins.[2]

Imagine a patriot like Jeremiah being called a traitor! Yet many a courageous leader who has dared to expose lies and call a nation to repentance has been called a traitor and publicly abused.

A true Christian patriot isn't blind to the sins of the nation but seeks to deal with those sins compassionately and realistically. Both Jesus and Jeremiah were true patriots when it came to giving an honest diagnosis of the diseases of the "body politic" and offering the only correct solution. They didn't heal the wounds of the people slightly and say, "Peace, peace." They both recognized that a nation's greatest problem is not unemployment, inflation, or lack of defense; it's sin. The nation that doesn't deal with sin is wasting time and resources trying to solve national problems, which are only symptoms of the deeper problem, which is sin.

4. God's servants occasionally have their doubts and failings. Jeremiah was weak before God but bold before men. He wasn't afraid to tell God just how he felt, and he listened when God told him what he needed to do. Though he once came quite close to resigning his office, he stuck with it and continued to serve the Lord.

Jeremiah was a prophet of the heart. He wasn't content to give a message that dealt with surface matters; he wanted to penetrate the inner person and see the heart changed. He boldly told the people that the days would come when they wouldn't remember the ark or feel a need for it. In fact, the days would come when they would be part of a New Covenant that would be written on the heart and not on tables of stone. This was radical religion, but it was God's message just the same.

Any servant of God who tries to reach and change hearts is a candidate for sorrow and a sense of failure. But God knows our hearts and sustains us.

5. The important thing isn't success; it's faithfulness. By today's human standards of ministry, Jeremiah was a dismal failure. He preached to the same people for over forty years, and yet few of them believed him or obeyed his message. He had few friends who stood with him and encouraged him. The nation he tried to save from ruin abandoned their God and plunged headlong into disaster. His record wouldn't have impressed the candidate committee of most missions or the pastoral search committee of the average church.

Jeremiah may have thought he had failed, but God saw him as a faithful servant, and that's all that really counts. "Moreover it is required in stewards that one be found faithful" (1 Cor. 4:2, NKJV). He could have quit, but he didn't. As V. Raymond Edman used to say, "It's always too soon to quit."

6. The greatest reward of ministry is to become like Jesus Christ. When Jesus asked His disciples who people said He was, they replied, "Some say John the Baptist, some Elijah, and others Jeremiah or one of the prophets" (Matt. 16:14, NKJV). What a compliment it would be to have people say, "Jesus Christ is like you!"

The similarities between Jesus and Jeremiah are interesting. Their approaches to teaching and preaching were similar, using "action sermons" and a great deal of imagery from everyday life and from nature. Both spoke out against the commercial "surface" religion practiced in the temple. Both were accused of being traitors to their people, and both suffered physically, even being arrested, beaten, and confined. Both wept over Jerusalem. Both were rejected by their relatives. Both knew what it was to be misunderstood, lonely, and rejected. Both emphasized the need for faith in the heart, and both rejected the mere "furniture" of religion that was external and impotent.

I could go on, but the point is obvious: Jeremiah became like Jesus because he shared "the fellowship of His sufferings" (Phil. 3:10). In the furnaces of life, Jeremiah was "conformed to the image of [God's] Son" (Rom. 8:29). Jeremiah may not have realized that this process was going on in his life, and he might have denied it if it were pointed out to him, but the transformation was going on just the same.

7. *God is King, and the nations of the world are under His sovereign control.* Nothing catches God by surprise. The nations that defy Him and disobey His Word eventually suffer for it. People who claim to know Him but who refuse to obey also suffer for it. In fact, the greater the light, the greater the responsibility. No nation was blessed the way God blessed the people of Israel, but that blessing brought chastening because they sinned against a flood of light.

It's a solemn responsibility for a people to claim to know God and profess to do His will. It isn't enough for a nation to put "In God We Trust" on its currency, to mention God in its pledge to the flag, or to "tip the hat to God" by quoting the Bible in political campaign speeches. It's *righteousness,* not religion, that exalts a nation. What pleases the Lord is that we "do justly . . . love mercy . . . and . . . walk humbly with [our] God" (Micah 6:8).

The same Lord who enabled Jeremiah can enable us.
The same world that opposed Jeremiah will oppose us.
It's time for God's people to be decisive.

NOTES

Chapter 1

1. G. Campbell Morgan, *Studies in the Prophecy of Jeremiah* (Westwood, N.J.: Fleming H. Revell, 1961), 19.

2. It's not likely that Jeremiah's father was the Hilkiah who found the Book of the Law during the repairing of the temple (2 Kings 22). In the Old Testament, there are several other Hilkiahs mentioned. The name was popular, particularly among the priests and Levites. If Jeremiah's father had been that close to the king, some of the prestige might have rubbed off on his son, but that doesn't seem to have happened.

3. I'm not discounting the fact that a priest's ministry was demanding in that he might disobey God and lose his life. He had to dress properly (Ex. 28:42-43), keep his hands and feet clean while serving (Ex. 30:20-21; Lev. 22:9), do his job carefully (Num. 4:15-20; 18:3), and always seek to glorify God (Lev. 16:13); otherwise, God's judgment could fall on him.

4. The ways of providence are sometimes puzzling. Hezekiah was a godly king, yet his son Manasseh was ungodly. Manasseh's son Amon, who reigned only two years, was as ungodly as his father (2 Kings 21:20-22); but Amon's son Josiah was a godly man. Yet Josiah's son, Jehoahaz, who reigned only three months, was ungodly like his grandfather. I suppose we must take into consideration both the influence of the mothers and of the court officials in charge of educating the princes.

5. The priestly city of Anathoth was located in the tribe of Benjamin (Josh. 21:18) and was about an hour's walk from Jerusalem. The priests would live in their own homes and travel to Jerusalem when their time came to minister in the temple. Contrary to the Law, there were also "local shrines" at which some of the priests served, making it convenient for the people who didn't want to go all the way to Jerusalem.

6. Josiah made the mistake of rashly getting involved at the battle of Carchemish, where Pharaoh Necho of Egypt was engaging the army of Assyria. Pharaoh Necho had warned Josiah to mind his own business, but the king persisted and was slain at Megiddo (2 Chron. 35:20-25).

7. Since many of the nobles, key leaders in the land, had already been deported to Babylon, the king was left with a weak staff. But it's doubtful that stronger men would have made any difference in his character or actions.

8. Compare God's call of Moses (Ex. 3–4) and Gideon (Jud. 6), and note how the Lord is patient with His servants and does all He can to encourage their faith. God still likes to use the most unlikely instruments to get His work done in this world, and for good reason: "That no flesh should glory in His presence" (1 Cor. 1:29).

9. God said of the Jews, "You only have I known of all the families of the earth" (Amos 3:2). Certainly God is acquainted with all the nations and knows what they do, but Israel is the only nation in history to have a special covenant relationship with the Lord God, and God chose them wholly by His grace (Deut. 4:32-37; 7:7-8). God said of Abraham, "For I know him" (Gen. 18:19), meaning, "I have chosen him."

10. The promise of His presence was given to Isaac (Gen. 26:1-3, 24); Jacob (Gen. 28:15; 31:3; 46:1-4); Moses (Ex. 3:12; 33:14); Joshua (Deut. 31:7-8; Josh. 1:5; 3:7; 6:27); Gideon (Jud. 6:15-16); Jeremiah (Jer. 1:8, 19; 20:11); and to the church (Matt. 28:19-20; Heb. 13:5-6). See also Isaiah 41:10; 43:5.

11. See Jeremiah 4:6; 6:1, 22; 10:22; 13:20; 15:12; 25:9; 47:2; 50:3, 9, 41; 51:48. The invading Babylonian army is compared to a boiling pot (1:14-15), a marauding lion (4:7), and a flooding river (47:2).

12. Henry David Thoreau, *Walden* (Princeton, N.J.: Princeton University Press, 1971), 326.

Chapter 2

1. National Fast-Day Proclamation, March 30, 1863.

2. The break at Jeremiah 3:6 indicates that two messages are recorded in these chapters, the first from 2:1 to 3:5, and the second from 3:6 to 6:30. Later, Jeremiah's messages were written down by his secretary Baruch, but King Jehoiakim burned the scroll. So Jeremiah dictated them again and added new messages to the book (Jer. 36).

3. The NIV seeks to convey this thought, and to some extent so does the NASB. Jeremiah was a master of imagery. You can't read his book without seeing pictures. This is a good example for all preachers and teachers of the Word to follow.

4. The word translated "kindness" in the KJV ("devotion," NIV) describes the grace and unfailing love of the Lord toward His people. It involves not just love but also the loyalty and faithfulness that are a part of true love. Israel was unfaithful to her husband and turned to idols. Today, believers who love the world are guilty of spiritual adultery (James 4:4), and local churches must beware of losing their "honeymoon love" for the Lord (Rev. 2:4-5; 2 Cor. 11:1-4).

5. The Prophet Isaiah used a similar image in Isaiah 8:5-8, warning King Ahaz that if he trusted Assyria, that nation would overflow like a turbulent river and destroy Judah. The quiet waters of Shiloah ("peace") flowed from the Gihon spring to the Pool of Siloam in Jerusalem (2 Chron. 32:30) and represented God's provision for His people (Ps. 46:4).

6. See Jeremiah 2:19; 3:6, 8, 11-12, 14, 22; 5:8; 8:5; 14:7; 21:22; 31:22; 49:4; 50:6; Hosea 11:7; 14:4.

7. According to the KJV and NASB, the "breaking of the yoke" in Jeremiah 2:20 refers to the Exodus when God set the Jews free (Lev. 26:13); but the NIV translates it "you broke off your yoke," referring to the nation's rebellion against God. Jeremiah 5:5 uses "breaking the yoke" to describe rebellion against God's will (see 31:18). The yoke is a recurring image in Jeremiah's writings (see especially 27–28, as well as 30:8; 51:23; Lam. 1:14; 3:27).

8. The KJV reads "the imagination of their evil hearts," based on the view that the Hebrew word comes from a root that means "to observe, to contemplate," hence, "to imagine." But the Hebrew word probably comes from a root that means "to be firm, to be hard."

9. Verse 4 of Charles Wesley's "O for a Thousand Tongues."

10. There was also sexual sin, for the pagan rites usually included consorting with prostitutes, both male and female. Idolatry and immorality often go together (Rom. 1:18ff).

11. Some of the hill shrines were devoted to Jehovah, but the Law

prohibited the Jews from sacrificing at any place other than in the temple (see Lev. 17:1-7; Deut. 12:1-16).

12. The NIV translates Jeremiah 3:14 "for I am your husband," for the Hebrew word for "husband" is the same as *baal* and means "lord." Baal was the Canaanite rain god that the Jews worshiped so as to have good crops. Therefore, there's a play on words here. "You are worshiping the false God Baal," says the prophet, "when your true baal—husband—is the Lord."

13. Jeremiah wasn't accusing God of deceiving the people, because God cannot lie (Titus 1:2; Num. 23:19). He was perplexed that God would even allow the false prophets to deliver their deceptive messages and lead the people into a false security that would be their undoing. But if people don't want to obey the truth, they will accept lies (2 Thes. 2:10-12). This is the second of fourteen personal prayers recorded in Jeremiah, the first being 1:6 (see 9:1-6; 10:23-25; 12:1-4; 14:7-9, 19-22; 15:15-18; 16:19-20; 17:12-18; 18:18-23; 20:7-18; 32:16-25). Three times, God instructed Jeremiah not to pray for the people (7:16; 11:14; 14:11).

14. In their attempt to prove that between Genesis 1:1 and 1:2 there was a "gap" during which God judged Lucifer and his angels, some scholars have used Jeremiah 4:23ff, building their case mainly on the phrase "without form and void" (KJV). But this passage refers to the invasion of the Babylonian army, not Genesis 1. Furthermore, if this passage does refer to Genesis 1, then we must believe in a pre-Adamic race who lived in cities; and yet Adam is called "the first man" (1 Cor. 15:45).

15. See also Psalm 48:6; Isaiah 13:8; 21:3; 26:17-18; 66:7; Micah 4:9-10; Hosea 13:13; 1 Thessalonians 5:3; Matthew 24:8; Mark 13:8; Romans 8:22; Galatians 4:19, 27.

16. They are: the search (Jer. 5:1-6), the soiled belt (13:1-11), the unwed prophet (16:1-9), the potter (18:1-12), the broken vessel (19:1-15), the yokes (27–28), the purchased field (32:1-15), the wine party (35:1-19), the stones (43:8-13), and the sunken scroll (51:59-64). You also find "action sermons" in the Book of Ezekiel. Whenever people become so spiritually dull that they can't hear and understand God's Word, the Lord graciously stoops to their level and dramatizes the message.

17. For "the remnant" in Jeremiah, see 23:3; 31:7; 39:9; 40:11; 41:16; 42:2, 15, 19; 43:5; 44:12, 14, 28.
18. The phrase "ask for the old paths" (6:16) is a favorite of people who oppose changes in the church and want to maintain a sterile and boring status quo. But "the old ways" refer to God's truth as revealed in His Word, not to methods of ministry. Note that Jeremiah gave two instructions: "stand in the old ways" and "walk in the good way." We stand on His truth in order to make progress in His work. The old Youth for Christ slogan comes to mind: "Geared to the times but anchored to the Rock."

Chapter 3

1. Thoreau wrote this in his journal on September 2, 1851.
2. These false prophets may have based their deceptive message on God's deliverance of Jerusalem in the days of Hezekiah (2 Kings 18–19; Isa. 37). But Hezekiah was a godly king who listened to the Word of God from the Prophet Isaiah, prayed to God for help, and sought to honor the Lord.
3. The Hebrew word translated "refuse" means "dung, manure," and Jeremiah used it again in 9:22, 16:4, and 25:33. What a tragedy that people who could have been children of God ended up manure in a garbage dump (see Mark 9:43-50).
4. Vance Havner, *It Is toward Evening* (Westwood, N.J.: Fleming H. Revell, 1968), 25. Vance Havner was himself a very witty man, and I always enjoyed his fellowship, but he knew how to use humor wisely to get his points across. In that same message, he writes, "Christians are never more ridiculous than when they attempt a religious version of worldly hilarity. It is always an embarrassing imitation that disgusts even the ungodly" (p. 27).
5. Jeremiah 9:22 pictures death as the "grim reaper" with the scythe in his hand, mowing people down like wheat in the field (see also Pss. 90:5; 103:14-16; Isa. 40:7; Job 5:26).
6. A.W. Tozer, *The Knowledge of the Holy* (New York: Harper and Row, 1961), 11.
7. Jeremiah's prayer reminds us of the "imprecatory psalms,"

such as Psalms 35, 69, 79, 109, 139, and 143. If we keep in mind that these prayers were an expression of *national* concern, not personal vengeance, asking God to keep His covenant promises to the nation (Gen. 12:1-3), then they become expressions of a desire for justice and the vindication of God's holy name. Their spirit is that of Paul's in Galatians 1:6-9 and the saints in heaven in Revelation 6:9-11 and 18:20-24.

Chapter 4

1. Ralph Waldo Emerson, "Self-Reliance," in *Essays.* Of course, Emerson used the word "man" generically, referring to either men or women.

2. Jeremiah 11:6 suggests that Jeremiah may have itinerated in Judah and taught the people the Law. This was one of the duties of the priests (2 Chron. 17:8-10; Ezra 7:10; Neh. 8:1-9).

3. Note the emphasis on *love* in the Book of Deuteronomy. The word is used twenty times, and love is presented as the motive for obedience to the Lord (6:4-5; 10:12; 11:1, 13, 22). The word "heart" is used nearly fifty times in Deuteronomy. In this "second edition" of the Law, Moses moved the emphasis from mere outward obedience to inward love and a desire to please God. Why we obey God is a mark of maturity in the Christian life.

4. Eugene Peterson, *Run with the Horses* (Downers Grove, Ill.: InterVarsity, 1983), 61.

5. See my book *Why Us? When Bad Things Happen to God's People* (Old Tappan, N.J.: Fleming H. Revell, 1984) for a discussion of this problem from a biblical/pastoral point of view. Other helpful books are: *In God's Waiting Room* by Lehman Strauss (Radio Bible Class); *The Paradox of Pain* by A.E. Wilder Smith (Harold Shaw); *Through the Fire* by Joseph M. Stowell (Victor); *Where Is God When It Hurts* by Philip Yancey (Zondervan); *The Problem of Pain* by C.S. Lewis (Macmillan); and *Surprised by Suffering* by R.C. Sproul (Tyndale). See also *Be Patient,* my study of the Book of Job (Victor).

The Old Testament system of rewards and punishments was suited to Israel in their "spiritual childhood" (Gal. 4:1-7), but it was never meant to be God's permanent arrangement for believers today. Jesus lived a perfect life and yet He suffered greatly, and nowhere in the New Testament is the church promised immunity from suffering. Quite the contrary is true: "Yes, and all who desire to live godly in Christ Jesus will suffer persecution" (2 Tim. 3:12, NKJV).

6. Hugh Black, *Listening to God* (London: Fleming H. Revell Co., 1906), 282.

7. See his essay "The Romance of Rhyme" in his book *Fancies versus Fads.*

8. The statement in Jeremiah 12:8 that God "hated" His inheritance means that He had to treat them as though they were not His beloved. He withdrew His love by abandoning them to their enemies. God's love for His people is unconditional, but their enjoyment of that love is conditional (see 2 Cor. 6:17-18; John 14:21-24).

9. The big question relating to this "action sermon" is, Where did it take place? The Euphrates was 350 miles from Anathoth, and that would mean four journeys of four months each for the prophet (Ezra 7:8-9). Could he make four such trips during such turbulent times? And how significant would his actions be to the people of Judah if he performed them hundreds of miles away? The Hebrew text of Jeremiah 13:4 reads *Perath,* which is the Hebrew word for the Euphrates, but some scholars think it refers to the town of Parah about three miles from Anathoth (Josh. 18:23), or that perhaps it is an abbreviation for Ephrata, the name of Bethlehem, located only five or six miles from Jerusalem. However, if Jeremiah did travel twice to Babylon, it would have made a tremendous impression on the people of Judah when he returned home with his ruined garment. He then could have preached the message that the garment symbolized.

10. The proverb speaks of wineskins, but the Hebrew word means "wine jars." The image in Jeremiah 13:14 is that of jars being dashed together and broken. The prophets used familiar sayings as springboards for teaching God's truth (see Jer. 17:11; 31:9; Ezek. 18:2).

11. Henri IV, King of France, said in his coronation address in 1589, "I hope to make France so prosperous that every peasant will

have a chicken in his pot on Sunday." In 1928, the American Republican party used "A chicken in every pot" as a campaign slogan.

Chapter 5

1. J. Wallace Hamilton, *The Thunder of Bare Feet* (Westwood, N.J.: Fleming H. Revell, 1964), 69.
2. John Henry Jowett, *The Preacher, His Life and Work* (New York: Harper & Brothers, 1921), 114.
3. The rainy season was from October to April, with the "early rains" coming in the spring and the "latter rains" in the autumn (Deut. 11:14; Jer. 8:3; 5:24). The "winter rains" began in November/December, the Hebrew month of Kislev.
4. The word "drought" in Jeremiah 14:1 is plural.
5. The three judgments of war, famine, and pestilence are mentioned often in Jeremiah (21:7, 9; 24:10; 27:8, 13; 29:17-18; 32:24, 36; 34:17; 38:2; 42:17, 22; 44:13; see also 5:12; 11:22; 14:13-18; 16:4; 18:21; 42:16; 44:12, 18, 27).
6. Jeremiah had predicted the invasion of the Babylonian army, but that invasion didn't occur until many years later. Since his prophecy didn't immediately come to pass, the people didn't take Jeremiah's messages too seriously. But God was watching over Jeremiah's word to perform it (1:12), and the disaster finally occurred.
7. For other references in Jeremiah to the Babylonian Captivity of Judah, see 9:16; 13:24; 16:13; 18:17; 30:11; 46:28.
8. God is holy and never has to repent of sin. The word is used to describe His "change of mind" when He determines not to send judgment. Humanly speaking, God seems to repent. From the divine point of view, however, God's purposes never change, though His providential workings do change.
9. On eating the word (Jer. 15:16); see Ezekiel 3:1-3; Revelation 10:9-10; Job 23:12. Unless the Word becomes a vital part of our inner being, we can't receive nourishment and grow in the spiritual life. This is what Jesus had in mind when He spoke about eating His flesh and drinking His blood (John 6:51-58). As we receive the written Word within, we are also receiving the living Word (1:14) and feeding on Christ.

10. Nine of the Ten Commandments are repeated in the New Testament epistles for believers to obey, but the Sabbath commandment isn't among them. The Sabbath was a special sign given to Israel (Ex. 31:12-18), not to the church. Believers are free to honor special days as they feel convicted by the Lord (Rom. 14:1-23; Col. 2:16-17) and must not judge one another. To make Sabbath-keeping a means of salvation or a mark of special spirituality is to go beyond what the Scriptures teach, and to equate the Sabbath with the New Testament Lord's Day is equally unbiblical. The Sabbath is identified with the Law: You work six days and then you have rest. The Lord's Day is identified with grace: You begin with a resurrected Christ and the works follow.

Chapter 6

1. J. Wilbur Chapman, *Revival Sermons* (New York: Fleming H. Revell, 1911), 231.
2. Charles E. Jefferson, *Cardinal Ideas of Jeremiah* (New York: Macmillan Co., 1928), 102.
3. The word translated "marred" is also used for the ruined girdle in Jeremiah 13:7 and 9. It means "to destroy or corrupt."
4. That God is sovereign over all the nations is proved by such Scriptures as Psalms 115:3; 135:6; Isaiah 46:9-11; Daniel 2:21, 4:17, 34-35; 7:14; Matthew 28:18; Acts 17:22-31; and Ephesians 1:22 to cite but a few.
5. The verb means "to empty" and is similar to the Hebrew word for jar. Perhaps Jeremiah had put water in the clay flask and then poured it out as he spoke these words. God would empty all the nation's plans and then break the nation that conceived them!
6. Three men named Pashur are found in this book: the son of Immer (Jer. 20:1), the son of Malchijah (21:1), and the father of Gedaliah (38:1). All three were enemies of Jeremiah and sought to silence his ministry. Whether the Pashur of 20:1 is the father of Gedaliah, we have no way of knowing for sure.
7. A century and a half before, Isaiah had predicted the Captivity and named Babylon as the aggressor (Isa. 6:11-13; 11:11-12; 39:6).

Therefore, any Jew who knew the Word of God would have recognized Jeremiah's witness as true. Jeremiah added the important facts about the seventy years' duration of the Captivity (Jer. 25).

Chapter 7

1. This is not the Pashur who persecuted Jeremiah (Jer. 20), although this Pashur later assisted in imprisoning Jeremiah and urging the king to kill him (Jer. 38). There's no evidence that Zephaniah the priest was opposed to the prophet. Zephaniah was eventually taken to Babylon and executed (2 Kings 25:18-21).

2. See Charles H. Dyer in *The Bible Knowledge Commentary, Old Testament* (Wheaton, Ill.: Victor Books, 1985), 1185.

3. The phrase "execute judgment in the morning" (Jer. 21:12) reminds us that court was held in the mornings at the city gates when it was still cool outside. But the phrase also suggests that the king needed to make justice the first priority of his day.

4. Obviously this message was delivered to King Jehoiakim before he died in 598 B.C. It's included in this section of Jeremiah's prophecy because it fits with the special messages to the four other kings. We've noted before that the Book of Jeremiah isn't assembled in chronological order. Chapters 21–24 focus especially on the royal house of David.

5. The fact that Jehoiakim "slept [rested] with his fathers" (2 Kings 24:6) is no proof that he had a decent burial. The phrase simply means that he joined his ancestors in death. Second Chronicles 36:6 indicates that Nebuchadnezzar bound Jehoiakim to take him to Babylon, which seems to contradict Jeremiah's prophecy. The easiest explanation is that the Babylonians intended to take Jehoiakim to Babylon, but he died. Therefore, they took Jehoiachin, his son and successor, instead (2 Kings 24:10-12). King Jehoiakim was not given a lavish state funeral and buried with the kings of Judah. His body was disposed of ignominiously somewhere outside the walls of Jerusalem, a shameful way for any man to be buried, especially a Jewish king.

6. Zerubbabel, a grandson of King Jehoiachin, was one of the Jew-

ish leaders who helped the exiles return to the land after the Captivity and reestablish their government and worship. He was a representative of the Davidic line though he didn't reign as a king. The Lord "reversed" the curse and said that Zerubbabel was to Him like a signet ring (Hag. 2:20-23), which meant he was chosen and precious to God.

7. The Hebrew word refers to the hot desert wind that smothers you, leaving you lifeless and ready to give up. In the KJV, the word is translated "terrible" in Lamentations 5:10 ("Our skin was black [hot] like an oven because of the terrible famine") and "horrible" in Psalm 11:6 ("Upon the wicked he shall rain . . . an horrible tempest").

Chapter 8

1. Quoted by Ann Landers in the column "Thoughts at Large" by Sidney J. Harris in *The Washington Post,* 12 Nov. 1979, B-7.

2. The name is also spelled Nebuchadrezzar. Famous leaders often had variant spellings to their names. Cf. Tiglath-Pileser (2 Kings 15:29), and Tiglath-Pilneser (1 Chron. 5:26).

3. Bible students don't agree on the dating of the seventy years of Captivity or even on whether the phrase "seventy years" should be considered a round number or be taken literally. From the beginning of the Babylonian invasion (606 B.C.) to the return of the Jewish remnant under Zerubbabel (536) is seventy years, but so is the period from the destruction of Jerusalem (587–586) to the completion of the second temple by the returned exiles (516). Daniel 9:1-2 seems to indicate that Daniel took the prophecy to mean seventy actual years.

4. While the main emphasis is on the world of Jeremiah's day, there may be a wider application of these words to the nations at the end of the age, for Jeremiah included "all the kingdoms of the world" (Jer. 25:26). In their messages, the prophets often began with a local situation and then used it as a springboard to describe something God would do in the end times.

5. Shaphan, Ahikam's father, is the scribe who delivered the Book of the Law to Josiah after Hilkiah found it in the temple (2 Kings

33). Shaphan had four sons, three of whom were friendly to Jeremiah: Ahikam, who saved his life (Jer. 26:24); Gemariah, who pleaded with King Jehoiakim not to burn Jeremiah's book (36:12, 25); and Elasah, who delivered Jeremiah's letter to the captive Jews in Babylon (29:1-3). The fourth son, Jaazaniah, was unfaithful to the Lord and worshiped idols in the temple (Ezek. 8:11). Ahikam's son Gedaliah became governor of Judah after the destruction of Jerusalem.

6. Don't be puzzled when you read the name "Jehoiakim" in verse 1 and the name "Zedekiah" in verses 3 and 12 (and see 28:1), because this event took place during the reign of Zedekiah. "Jehoiakim" in verse 1 appears to be the error of a copyist whose eyes may have read 26:1, which is almost identical to 27:1. The fact that the rest of the chapter names Zedekiah as king is ample evidence that "Jehoiakim" is a scribal error.

7. Some translations give the impression that the prophet wore more than one yoke and that he sent a yoke to each of the envoys of the five nations (Jer. 27:2-3). The word "yoke" is plural in the Hebrew because the yoke he wore was made of two pieces of wood, one in front of the neck and one at the back, held together by leather straps. "Make a yoke out of straps and crossbars" (NIV) is a good translation of verse 2. He sent *word* to the five kings that they were to submit to the authority of Nebuchadnezzar, and the yoke that he wore symbolized the prophet's message.

8. There were three deportations—in 605, 597, and 586—during which both people and treasures were taken to Babylon. Since Zedekiah ruled from 597 to 586, the false prophets were referring to the deportation in 605, when Daniel and his friends were taken to Babylon along with some of the temple treasures (Dan. 1:1-2).

9. It's profitable to compare Jeremiah's counsel to the exiles in Babylon with Peter's counsel to the "pilgrims and strangers" in the Roman Empire (1 Peter 2:11-17). Both men told the people to be good citizens and good witnesses and to do good works. Paul agreed with their approach when he wrote, "If it is possible, as much as depends on you, live peaceably with all men" (Rom. 12:18, NKJV).

Chapter 9

1. Charles E. Jefferson, *Cardinal Ideas of Jeremiah* (New York: Macmillan, 1928), 125.

2. Isaiah used the phrase "in that day" at least forty-four times, but Jeremiah only seven (4:9; 30:8; 39:16-17; 49:22, 26; 50:30). In chapters 12 to 14 of Zechariah, "in that day" is used nineteen times with reference to end-time events relating to the restoration of Israel and the return of the Lord.

3. Jesus designated the first part of the Tribulation as "the beginning of sorrows" (Matt. 24:8) which means "the beginning of birth-pangs." The Tribulation will bring pain to Israel and the nations of the world, but out of that pain will come the birth of the kingdom.

4. Visitors to the Holy Land visit Tel Aviv and various other "tells" and learn that the Hebrew word *tel* means "a mound of ruins." Cities devastated by war or natural calamities rarely relocated; the survivors simply rebuilt the city on the ruins of the old one, thus giving future archeologists something to do.

5. The ancient breach between Jews and Samaritans was healed when Philip the evangelist took the Gospel to Samaria and the believing Samaritans received the same gift of the Spirit as the Jews (Acts 8:5ff; 2:1-4). Later, the Gentiles would receive the gift (Acts 10:44-48). Thus, believing Jews, Samaritans, and Gentiles made up the body of Christ (Gal. 3:26-29).

6. We sometimes hear about the "ten lost tribes of Israel," and various groups claim the identification, but only God knows where all twelve tribes are in the world (Acts 26:7; James 1:1; Rev. 7).

7. How does this relate to Matthew's quotation? As Rachel died, she named her son *Ben-oni,* which means "son of my sorrow," but Jacob named him *Benjamin,* "son of my right hand" (Gen. 35:16-20). In His humiliation and suffering, Jesus Christ is "the man of sorrows," but in His exaltation and glory, He is the Son at God's right hand (Acts 2:22-36). Jacob made Bethlehem a burial place, but Jesus made it a birthplace! The Bethlehem mothers, bereft of their sons, wept in despair, but just as God's promises comforted Rachel, so their sacrifice would not be in vain. No matter how many ene-

mies try to destroy Israel, the nation will not perish, for their Messiah reigns and will come one day and deliver His people.

8. To defend this verse as a prediction of the virgin birth of Christ is an exercise in futility. The word for "woman" means "female" without reference to virginity. The nation is the only virgin mentioned in the context (Jer. 31:4, 21). There is no definite article in the text; it simply says "a female" and not "the woman." The Hebrew word translated "surround" (compass) has nothing to do with the conception of a child. It's possible that the statement is a Jewish proverb for an amazing and unthinkable thing.

9. Baruch may have had royal blood in his veins since his brother Seraiah was a staff officer in the king's service (Jer. 51:59, NIV), and such officials were usually princes. The fact that Seraiah went to Babylon with the king shows how important a man he was in the eyes of the Babylonians. The family of Neriah may have thought that Baruch gave up a bright future in order to serve with Jeremiah, but they were wrong. Many of the royal officers perished, but God protected Jeremiah and Baruch and provided for them (see Jer. 45). No doubt Baruch was an encouragement to the prophet, who was usually friendless and forsaken.

10. The statement goes back to Abraham (Gen. 18:14), and was also used by Moses (Num. 11:23) and Job (Job 42:2). Gabriel echoed it when he said to Mary, "For with God nothing shall be impossible" (Luke 1:37), and Jesus said, "With God all things are possible" (Matt. 19:26). Paul's testimony was "I can do all things through Christ who strengthens me" (Phil. 4:13, NKJV). Jeremiah discovered that God's character is faithful and His promises are true no matter how we feel or what our circumstances may be.

11. Good and godly Bible students disagree as to whether these "kingdom promises" are to be taken literally or interpreted in a "spiritual sense." If these promises are to be applied to the church today, it's difficult to understand what they mean and how they apply. I have therefore taken the approach that these promises will have their real fulfillment in the future kingdom. For further study, see *There Really Is a Difference* by Renald E. Showers (Friends of Israel); *Millennialism: The Two Major Views* by Charles L. Feinberg (Moody Press); *The Millennial Kingdom* by

John F. Walvoord (Dunham); and *Continuity and Discontinuity,* edited by John S. Feinberg (Crossway Books).

Chapter 10

1. Senator Shepherd said this during remarks made in the U.S. Senate on Dec. 18, 1914, as recorded in the *Congressional Record,* vol. 52, 338.
2. What was recorded is *revelation;* the way it was recorded is *inspiration.* Never confuse divine inspiration with the "human inspiration" of great writers like Shakespeare and Milton.
3. For example, eight men named Shelemiah are found in the Old Testament, so it was a popular name. Because of this, we can never be sure of family relationships.
4. John F. Kennedy, *Profiles in Courage* (New York: Harper & Row, 1955), 245.
5. The contradiction between Jeremiah 39:11-14 and 40:1-6 is only on the surface. When the Babylonians entered the city, they released Jeremiah and took him under their protective custody. He was free to move about and minister to the people. Apparently through some blunder, he was taken captive with the prisoners going to Ramah, but when the mistake was discovered, he was released and allowed to do as he pleased.
6. G. Campbell Morgan, *Studies in the Prophecy of Jeremiah* (Westwood, N.J.: Revell, 1961), 251.

Chapter 11

1. Dag Hammarskjold, *Markings* (New York: Alfred A. Knopf, 1965), 8.

Chapter 12

1. Quoted in *Miracle at Philadelphia,* by Catherine Drinker Bowen

(Boston: Little, Brown and Company, 1966), 126. Italics are in the original.

2. The phrase in the KJV "this is the day of the Lord" (Jer. 46:10) should not be interpreted to mean "the day of the Lord" which will occur in the end times. The battle Jeremiah described took place in 605 and is known as the Battle of Carchemish, named for a town on the Euphrates River.

3. The *New English Bible* translates it "King Bombast, the man who missed his moment."

4. The phrase "make a full end" is found in Jeremiah 4:27; 5:10, 18; 30:11; and Ezekiel 11:13. The NIV translates it "completely destroy." God knows how much discipline to give His people, and He never makes a mistake. He keeps His eye on the clock and His hand on the thermostat.

5. "Madmen" in Jeremiah 48:2 is the name of a Moabite city. It's not the English word for men who are mad.

Chapter 13

1. Dennis J. Hester, compiler, *The Vance Havner Quotebook* (Grand Rapids: Baker Book House, 1986), 124.

2. Some Hebrew scholars connect the name Nimrod with the word *marad*, which means "to rebel." Certainly the building of the Tower of Babel was an act of rebellion against the Lord. Nimrod chased and conquered other peoples the way a hunter chases and catches game.

3. King Hezekiah used a similar image (Isa. 38:12). Our lives are a weaving that one day will end, and God will cut it off the loom.

4. Some commentators see the hammer as Babylon, but Jeremiah 51:24 seems to require something or someone other than Babylon; otherwise Jeremiah would have used "you" instead of "they."

5. Remember, this didn't happen when Cyrus took Babylon, for his army was in the city before the Babylonians even knew it. He had diverted the waters of the Euphrates and entered under the gates. It was Alexander the Great whose army destroyed Babylon in 330.

6. Before the farmers threshed their grain, they would stamp down the earth to make sure it was hard. This may be the image here: God was stamping down the nation and preparing to cut them down like so much grain in the field.

7. The Jews often wanted to go back to Egypt, because there they had plenty of food and security, even though they were slaves. It's tragic when people sacrifice fulfillment for comfort.

Postlude

1. Dennis J. Hester, compiler, *The Vance Havner Quotebook* (Grand Rapids: Baker, 1986), 179.

2. Charles E. Jefferson, *Cardinal Ideas of Jeremiah* (New York: Macmillan, 1928), 192.

Chapter One

The Reluctant Prophet

(Jeremiah 1)

1. What is the worst job you can think of? What are some excuses you might use to try to get out of doing it?

2. Read Jeremiah 1. What was Jeremiah's objection to becoming a prophet?

3. What changed his attitude?

4. Although Jeremiah saw himself as a child, how did God see him? Why?

5. God used an almond branch, which blossoms early, to symbolize His watchfulness and a boiling pot to represent His impending judgment. What contemporary symbols do you think He might use to reveal Himself? Why?

6. What do you think would have been the worst part of Jeremiah's assignment? Why?

7. What would have been the best part? Why?

8. Given similar conditions today, would you be willing to stand for God against powerful opposition? Why or why not?

9. What resources does God give His people to help them deal with their doubts in difficult circumstances?

10. How can you use one of these resources this week?

Chapter Two

The Prophet Preaches
(Jeremiah 2–6)

1. How do you feel when you have to relay bad news to someone you care about?

2. God expected Jeremiah to pass along the bad news that judgment was coming. Read Jeremiah 2. What ten symbols represented God's rebellious people? How was each an apt description?

3. How do you think Jeremiah felt, calling his own people these awful names?

4. What do these negative symbols suggest about God's attitude toward the sinfulness of His people?

5. Skim Jeremiah 3 and 4. What do these chapters teach us about repentance?

6. Read Jeremiah 5. What do you learn about righteousness from the people's lack of it?

7. Read Jeremiah 6. What do you learn about retribution?

8. Why did Judah suffer so much?

9. What have you learned from Jeremiah's decisive message to Judah?

10. Read Jeremiah 5:1. How can one person who is decisive make a difference?

11. In what ways can you speak up for God?

Chapter Three

The Voice in the Temple

(Jeremiah 7–10)

1. If you were to attend a church for the first time this Sunday, how would you evaluate the strengths and weaknesses of the worship service?

2. Read Jeremiah 7:1–8:3. What did Jeremiah say about the false worship of his day?

3. Read Jeremiah 8:4-22. In exposing the false prophets, what did Jeremiah say about the people's refusal to obey God?

4. Skim Jeremiah 9. How were the people misusing their covenant relationship with God?

5. Skim Jeremiah 10. How did Jeremiah respond to the false gods the people worshiped?

6. What was the single worst offense the people of Judah committed? Why? When do you think their problem started?

7. Why were the people so unwilling to change their offensive worship habits even after Jeremiah's prophecy of the coming captivity?

8. Wiersbe asserts that "the remedy for idolatry is for us to get caught up in the majesty and grandeur of God, the true God, the living God, the everlasting King." How can you practice this truth this week?

Chapter Four

Voting with God
(Jeremiah 11–13)

1. Describe a situation when you found it difficult to stand with God. Why was it hard?

2. Read Jeremiah 11. Why did God remind the people of His covenant with them?

3. What was the consequence Jeremiah faced when he stood with God?

4. Even though Jeremiah took a bold stand for God, he still had questions about why God operated the way He did. Read Jeremiah 12:1-4. What were Jeremiah's specific concerns?

5. Do you think Jeremiah was disagreeing with God or trying to understand God's plan? Why?

6. What characterizes people who have God "always on their lips but far from their hearts"? (v. 2)

7. God's answer to Jeremiah appears in 12:5-17. What was God's plan?

8. Read Jeremiah 13. What object lessons did God use to help Jeremiah understand His way of thinking? What spiritual truth did each teach?

9. If God were to create an object lesson to remind you to stand boldly for Him, what would it be? Why?

Chapter Five

Sermons, Supplications, and Sobs

(Jeremiah 14–17)

1. When have you doubted God?

2. Read Jeremiah 14:1–15:9. What was the main point of Jeremiah's sermon to the people?

3. How did the people and the prophet respond?

4. How did God in turn respond to their prayers?

5. Read Jeremiah 15:10-21. How did Jeremiah feel about what God was going to do?

6. Did he have a right to feel the way he did? Why or why not?

7. If you had been in Jeremiah's place, how would you have liked God's response?

8. Read Jeremiah 16 and 17. What was the next opportunity God provided for Jeremiah to be decisive?

9. How did Jeremiah respond to it?

10. What specific sins of the people did Jeremiah point out?

11. How can you follow Jeremiah's example and be more decisive in an area of your life?

Chapter Six

The Prophet, the Potter, and the Policeman
(Jeremiah 18–20)

1. Describe an object that symbolizes your current spiritual condition. Explain the meaning of your object.

2. Read Jeremiah 18:1-17 and chapter 19. What objects did God use to represent the spiritual condition of His people? Why?

3. As Jeremiah continued to proclaim God's message of judgment to the people of Judah, his decisiveness to speak for God continued to be tested. Read Jeremiah 18:18-23 and chapter 20. How did the people make ministry harder for God's faithful messenger?

4. What do Jeremiah's prayers reveal about his feelings in this situation?

5. How would you have felt if you had been in Jeremiah's situation?

6. What hope did Jeremiah have in spite of his discouragement and despair?

7. What do you learn about prayer from Jeremiah's prayers in these chapters?

8. What practical steps can you take to keep from giving up on God when you're persecuted for speaking the truth?

Chapter Seven

Kings on Parade

(Jeremiah 21–24)

1. When has a trusted leader (i.e., political, religious, head of company) abused his or her power and betrayed your trust? How did you feel?

2. Jeremiah experienced the same kind of betrayal. Read Jeremiah 21. What messages from God did Jeremiah give King Zedekiah and the people of Judah?

3. How might the king have reacted to this message?

4. How would God's message have affected the people?

5. Read Jeremiah 22. Compare the messages Jeremiah proclaimed to the kings. What truths did he repeat?

6. Read Jeremiah 23:1-8. How did Jeremiah contrast the righteous branch, or Messiah, with the current rulers of God's people?

7. How does this prophecy affect us today?

8. Read Jeremiah 23:9-40. What sins of the false prophets did Jeremiah expose?

9. Read Jeremiah 24. What did God teach Jeremiah through the vision of the baskets of figs?

10. To whom are you a leader, or whom do you have the ability to influence? How can living more decisively for God affect the people you influence?

Chapter Eight

Facing Truth and Fighting Lies
(Jeremiah 25–29)

1. Would you rather hear bad news that is the absolute truth, and half-truths or lies that cushion the bad news for you? Why?

2. As Jeremiah proclaimed God's truth, other prophets told the people lies. Read the following passages and contrast Jeremiah's message with those of Judah's false prophets:

- threats from Babylon: 25:8-10; 26:10-11
- length of captivity: 25:11; 28:1-3
- loss of the temple furnishings: 27:19-22; 28:3
- return of King Jehoiachin: 27:24-27; 28:4
- yoke of Babylon: 27:2-11; 28:10-11
- results of prophesying: 26:7-16, 24; 28:12-17; 29:21
- plans for living in Babylon: 25:8-10; 29:8-9; 28:3; 29:4-7

3. How would you characterize Jeremiah's messages? The false prophets' messages?

4. Why were these messages so different?

5. Read Jeremiah 29:1-14. What hope did Jeremiah give the people?

6. How can this hope help us when we struggle with listening to and obeying God's truth?

7. What are some half-truths or lies that religious people proclaim today?

8. How can you protect yourself from buying into these lies?

Chapter Nine

The God Who Makes Things New

(Jeremiah 30–33)

1. What is an investment you have made for the future?

2. Jeremiah was instructed to make an investment too. Read Jeremiah 30 and 31. What hope for the future did God give Jeremiah and His people?

3. Read Jeremiah 32:1–32:25. What reasons did Jeremiah have for being pessimistic and/or giving up? For being optimistic?

4. If you were in Jeremiah's place, weighing the good against the bad, how would you feel? Why?

5. What object lesson did God instruct Jeremiah to perform to confirm that everything would eventually be OK?

6. Read Jeremiah 32:16-44. What was the overriding theme of Jeremiah's prayer?

7. How did God affirm that Judah's situation wasn't totally lost?

8. What aspects of your own future would you feel more secure about if you focused on God's previous faithfulness rather than the fear of the unknown?

9. Read Jeremiah 33. In addition to promising to restore order back to the land of Judah, what else did God promise Jeremiah?

10. How does this passage relate to our futures?

Chapter Ten

Contemporary Events and Eternal Truths

(Jeremiah 34–39; 52)

1. If you were going to write a want ad for a "full-service" servant, what characteristics/qualifications would you include? Why?

2. Jeremiah was a full-service servant. Let's see how he demonstrated this quality in contrast to others who were self-centered. Skim Jeremiah 34–38. How did Jeremiah demonstrate his complete commitment to God?

3. What other examples of commitment to God are noted in these chapters?

4. How did King Zedekiah and others demonstrate self-centered behavior?

5. What are the benefits of living a life of consistent commitment to God?

6. What are some of the dangers of attempting to appear spiritual while doing as little as possible?

7. Skim Jeremiah 39 and 52. What were the consequences of Zedekiah's decisions and lifestyle?

8. What does a full-fledged commitment to a consistent, God-pleasing lifestyle look like today?

9. What can you do this week to demonstrate this kind of commitment?

Chapter Eleven

Tragedy Follows Tragedy

(Jeremiah 40–45)

1. What are some ways people respond to tragedy?

2. After Babylon conquered Judah, the Book of Jeremiah records several responses to tragedy, most of which didn't work. Skim Jeremiah 40:7–43:13. Why did Jeremiah stay in Judah instead of going to Babylon?

3. How did Ishmael and Johanan respond to the tragedy of the fall of Jerusalem? What happened as a result?

4. What did Jeremiah's object lesson teach the Jewish remnant who went to Egypt?

5. Read Jeremiah 44. How did the Jewish remnant respond to the tragedy? Why?

6. Of deceit, hypocrisy, and idolatry, which do you think is the worst response to tragedy? Why?

7. Why weren't the people of Judah more mature in their relationship with God and in response to tragedy?

8. Read 40:1-6 and 45:1-5. How were Baruch's and Jeremiah's responses different from the others you've just read about?

9. When tragedy strikes in your life, how do you usually respond?

10. In light of this study, what changes would you like to make as you respond to tragedy in the future?

Chapter Twelve

God Speaks to the Nations
(Jeremiah 46–49)

1. What evidences can you cite that demonstrate God's involvement in the world?

2. In Jeremiah 46–49, Jeremiah recorded God's prophecies concerning the nations. Read the following sections, and summarize God's judgment on each nation:
   - Egypt: chapter 46
   - Philistia: chapter 47
   - Moab: chapter 48
   - Ammon: 49:1-6
   - Edom: 49:7-22
   - Damascus: 49:23-27
   - Arabia: 49:28-33
   - Elam: 49:34-39

3. Throughout these judgments, what hope did God give Israel?

4. What do these chapters teach about God?

5. Which of the sins mentioned in these chapters are prevalent in our nation today?

6. What can you do to encourage people to repent of sin in order to avoid judgment?

Chapter Thirteen

Babylon Is Fallen!

(Jeremiah 50–51)

1. What's the worst judgment you can imagine?

2. Read Jeremiah 50 and 51. Why did God declare war on Babylon?

3. Describe Babylon's judgment and God's victory.

4. Why was God's judgment of Babylon so harsh?

5. In dealing with sinful people, why would God use others who are even more sinful to turn them back to Himself?

6. What lessons can we learn from this dramatic description of the fall of Babylon?

7. Looking back on the Book of Jeremiah, what have you learned about being decisive from this study?

8. Think of an ongoing challenge you face. Read Jeremiah 1:4-10. How can these verses help you face that challenge instead of running away from it?